Decoding Jesus

A Comparison between John Calvin and Ellen G. White's Views

Dr. PP Jones, Th.D

Strategic Book Publishing and Rights Co.

Strategic Book Publishing and Rights Co.
12620 FM 1960, Suite A4-507
Houston, TX 77065
www.sbpra.com

ISBN: 978-1-62857-742-6

Design: Dedicated Book Services (www.netdbs.com)

Dedication

I dedicate this book to the entire International Community, especially the Church of Christ. This is in honor and commemoration of the late President Nelson Mandela. Although Mr. Mandela did not publicly profess to be a Christian, the major ideals he had internalized and epitomized through his life, are in concert and symphonic harmony with the meandering stream flowing through this book—creation, reconciliation, renewal and fulfillment.

Preface

What is *Decoding Jesus* about? While the world around us is cluttered with records concerning Jesus—this book—is not just one of the many. In a world of internet speeds that are immensely fast, lingering unobtrusive drones replacing fast flying jets, fast paced wavelike changes in global economics making the rich richer and the poor poorer, competing churches losing members in droves, politics polluted by entrenched self-interest and populations polarized to the hilt—Jesus remains one of the most intriguing, fascinating and controversial 'topics' of all times.

Many in secularized societies, especially those currently in the Western world, may often feel repulsed to any reference of Christianity or Christians in general. The reasons are overwhelmingly many. Some of these reasons stretch from outdated packages of the Christian message that is not liberating to people's already dreadful existence to scandals involving many in the Christian world. For many the whole story of religion does not make sense. Notwithstanding these and other reasons, a large portion of people in secularized societies, while they may not be attracted to Christians, their churches and their messages ,they are nevertheless attracted to the *man of Galilee—Jesus.*

In various segments of the modern world, marketers know that Jesus sells, as long as the package in which he is provided is cleverly presented. The world of Hollywood also knows that. Mel Gibson made an instant billion US dollars with his acclaimed movie *The Passion of Christ.* Prolific writers know that the story of Jesus carries a fascinating mystery in itself. It is in this regard that Dan Brown tapped into the wide spread interest into the mystery of Jesus. He purportedly moved many people's minds with the publishing of his controversial *Da Vinci Code.* Conclusion—one can become a billionaire by pretending to decipher the mystery of Jesus as long as the book is well written and impressively thick. Millions of people are still interested.

What emerges in this book, not as thick as the learned tomes of many, is a deciphering of who Jesus is in the practicalities of our lives and the practicalities of the life of God. Jesus fits as a driving force into the threesome of God, human beings and the natural cosmic world. In this sense as part of the threesome of God, human beings and the natural cosmic world, Jesus comes to the fore in the grand acts of God in the Judeo-Christian Bible depicted as creation, reconciliation (the cross and the resurrection), renewal (the Holy Spirit at Pentecost) and fulfillment at the end of times.

The method of my enquiry is through a careful comparative analytical study of Ellen G. White and John Calvin. Why I chose John Calvin and Ellen G. White as comparative partners in *Decoding Jesus*—is why you should embark with me on this journey.

The project began while I was a student at Oakwood University in Huntsville Alabama, in the fall of 1994. It grew into something thicker and fuller when I had to write a paper at Southern Adventist University, Tennessee in 1998. More mature and fulfilling it became—while I was pursuing my *Master* and *Doctor* degrees in systematic theology, through the University of South Africa from 1999-2010. Thereafter, I continued probing and delving yet deeper and incessantly on *who*, Jesus really is and how he relates to God, human beings and the natural created environment.

Ellen White paradoxically—like Jesus—is a subject of controversy within the global landscape of the churches. Some call her a prophet, while others claim that she was just a devotional writer and someone engaged in practicing everyday faith experience. What is astonishing is that none call her a theologian. In this book, we discover that White, like Calvin—not regarded as a real theologian by many—had a systematic way of doing theology in the drawing patterns of faith about God, human beings and the natural created environment within the broad ambience of the biblical historical timeline. White's way of doing theology was an *anti-speculative* approach using the Judeo-Christian Bible as an ambience in which she herself was closely engaged in her reflection on God, human beings and the natural created cosmos. This engagement in experiential faith patterns is what she has written down and worked out in her writings. The name that commentators gave to Calvin's writings as *pastoral dogmatics* could very aptly be attached to White's writings. White's contribution to the global theological scene is far more unique and surprising than what people inside and outside the Seventh Day Adventist world would acknowledge.

Prologue

Some people may ask the question, why would one discuss and compare John Calvin—the major trendsetter and co-founder of the large group of mainline Reformed churches with a controversial and nonconformist, Ellen G. White, the main trendsetter and co-founder of the Seventh-day Adventist Church, that is still regarded by many as a church on the fringes of the global mainline church landscape. It is common knowledge to Calvinists and Seventh Day Adventists that the 16th century John Calvin and the 19th century Ellen G. White, living almost three hundred years apart, generally held very divergent points of view. What is not well known is that they have been sharing similar views in vital parts of their approaches.

One of the major characteristics they shared is their continuous defiance of the *scholastics'* speculative way of reflection and contemplation about God, human beings and the whole of creation. Calvin and White used the Judeo-Christian Bible from Genesis to Revelation as their main ambience of reflection, their main expanded spatial bubble of reflection about God, human beings and the entire created cosmos. They both shunned speculation outside the dynamics of the biblical historical timeline in which they traced the four grand acts, that is the operational dimensions of God: creation; reconciliation (Redemption - the cross and resurrection); renewal (The Holy Spirit at Pentecost) and fulfillment (The final consummation or end of time). While Calvin emphasized the first two more: creation and reconciliation (the cross and resurrection), White's approach is more dynamically extended to all four: creation; reconciliation; renewal and fulfillment.

Along the journey we undertake, the 'Trinity' is dealt with in passing, as one of the center point around which many discussions revolve. Later on we alarmingly notice how Calvin experienced problems in his employment of the historical timeline of the Bible as his main ambience of reflection on God's grand acts around which the threesome of God, human beings and the cosmic world continuously revolve. He also contradictorily held on to the traditional speculative dogma of the Trinity with its speculative overtones of a trinitarian God acting above God's grand acts. Ellen G. White wrote over 100,000 transcribed pages set in periodical articles, typewritten manuscripts consisting of letters and documents and tracts and letters that were handwritten in journals. Her voluminous-writings comprise more than 130 books currently in print. Yet strangely enough, —in the vast sea of her writings—the word—'Trinity'—is missing. In all of her voluminous work she almost bypasses the discussion of the Trinity. Later on towards the end of her life she seemingly makes a careful 'U-turn' but still—did not mention the word 'Trinity.' The furthest she went was to make mention of '*the three living persons of the heavenly trio*.' In this work, her conspicuous omission of the old edged word 'Trinity' and by-passing of the traditional notion of the Trinity, could be regarded as a smoking gun!

In *Decoding Jesus* we deal with: *how Jesus could be both God and man? If he was omnipresent as God is, how could he have left heaven and be contained in a virgin's womb? What happened to his divinity at the incarnation? When he was of adolescent age or at any other time, did he use his divine power to benefit himself to be of better advantage over other humans? What happened to his divinity when he calmed the storm at The Sea of Galilee? What was his divinity doing when he made his triumphant entry into Jerusalem? And what happened to his divinity while he was dying on the cross of Golgotha? What happened to his humanity after he had risen and ascended to heaven? Where is his human nature, now? What will happen to his human nature in eternity?*

During the cause of our journey, we notice that Calvin and White's Christological method of allowing 'God to stay God' and 'humans to stay human' in an *interactional substantialist* sense in Christ, denotes a divergent view from the *trans-substantialist* view (historically linked to the Roman Catholic Church) in which the human Jesus is in a *sacramental-sacred* way transformed into 'a divine human being.' Calvin and White's *interactional-substantialist* view also differed from the Lutheran *consubstantialist* view, whereby the human Jesus is permeated and diffused by his divinity, therefore becoming 'the human God.' It is of interest here that the majority of evangelical Christians in the world without knowing tend to follow the 'divine Jesus nestled in the heart view' that derives more from Luther than from Calvin's views. In White's view of the identity of the dual natures of Jesus Christ, it is revealed that we sometimes see his *quiescent divinity* (allowing more of his humanness to show) and at other times his *active divinity* (allowing more of his divine nature to be revealed).

On quite a number of important points emphasized in the global array of mainline church theologies White's faith studies are an immense contribution, demonstrating that it is not always the mighty world of the recognized big theologians that annunciate the changes of an era—but the seemingly powerless on the edges—reads sometimes the signs of changes of an era far better.

Contents

CHAPTER 1

Concrete Biblical Reflection or Speculative Theologizing?

1.1 The First Problem Setting: God's Grand Acts of Creation, Reconciliation, Renewal, and Fulfillment Open to Biblical Reflection or Speculative Theologizing?

In the first problem setting, John Calvin and Ellen G. White's operational uses of God's grand acts of creation, reconciliation (redemption), renewal, and fulfillment (consummation), as embodied in the *salvation-historical corpus of the biblical texts* from Genesis to Revelation, is investigated and portrayed. This kind of salvation-historical approach embodied in their writings, sayings, and doings revolves around a divine history embedded in the portrayal of the whole array of God's grand acts in the Judeo-Christian Bible, with God as the all-initiating agent. This divine history is of such a special kind that all of world history outside the biblical depiction of divine history is reliant on the biblical rendition of real and genuine history.

An outstanding feature of their kind of theology is that they continuously *connect and describe in their concrete reflection and discussion* the threesome of God, human beings, and the natural cosmic environment in each of God's grand acts portrayed as divine history in the Judeo-Christian Bible. Their concrete kind of faith patterning and theorizing is way beyond the theologies of medieval scholastics and modern orthodoxy, which discuss and reflect on God while underemphasizing the discussion and reflection on human beings and the natural cosmic environment. The great theologies of medieval scholastics and modern orthodoxy not only underemphasize the domains of human beings and the natural environment, but they fully endorsed the ancient philosophical threesome of God, human beings, and the natural environment to be portrayed as separate and divided avenues of reflection and discussion. In this separated and divided sense, the reflection in the theological avenue of discussion revolved around the notions of faith and love closely and directly linked to God. In the anthropological avenue of human beings and cosmological avenue of nature, the reflection was done in the embrace of human reason and common sense remotely and indirectly linked to God. Superseding this separated and divided scheme, Calvin and White continually emphasize the simultaneous close connection and radical difference between God, human beings, and the natural cosmic environment in their reflection and discussion of divine history portrayed in the Bible.

One possible reason why Calvin and White were not regarded as theologians in the classical mound is their insistence on treating God, human beings, and nature as a "reflexive coherence" within the realm of biblically portrayed divine history. It is significant that they do not have separate anthropologies or cosmologies. Calvin and White's dealings with divine history as portrayed in the Bible are expressed in their writings, sayings, and doings, and in their intrinsic aversion to go beyond and above the divinely set range of the grand acts of God. What could generally be described as their salvation-historical approaches comprise the divinely set range of biblically portrayed grand acts of God continuously enveloped in the mystery of the close connection and radical difference of God, human beings, and the natural cosmic environment.

This notion deals with the difference between the essence-seeking approach of *scholastic and orthodox types* of theology and Calvin and White's salvation-historical approach in which theological reflection is conducted by following the sequence of God's grand acts of creation, reconciliation, renewal, and fulfillment, as portrayed by the biblical texts from Genesis to Revelation. Calvin and White, while differing in many respects, have one major thing in common, and that is not to follow the typical scholastic theological approach of speculating about the essences of God, human beings, and nature as separate entities above and outside God's grand acts as portrayed in the Bible. Moreover, it is significant that they also do not make use of scholasticism's bifocal speculative treatment of reflecting in an either/or way on the "inside" and "outside" of God, human beings, or the natural cosmic world. Although, when they discuss God or an aspect of God, human beings, and nature, they do not always explicitly carry the same weight of God in their reflections.

The notion of the *Trinity* is another case in point. The question with regard to Calvin is how a Trinitarian God who operates beyond the grand acts of God's creation, reconciliation, renewal, and fulfillment could be combined, harmonized, and radically built into these grand acts. In Calvin's writings, sayings, and doings, the notion of the Trinity plays a less important role than his main reflexive realms of creation and redemption covered and undergirded by his divine salvation storyline. Interestingly, the notion of the Trinity is an intrinsic part of the scholastic speculative approach. In the past early centuries, problems with the notion of a Trinitarian God emerged in various theological avenues. The result of the latter was an awareness of increasing problems with the notion of the Trinity that spilled over into the Reformed and Presbyterian world. Various new approaches to problems in the sixteenth-century Reformation and Calvin's work are detected—one of which is a seeming contradiction between his acceptance of the notion of the Trinity and his strong emphasis on the divine history embedded in the grand acts of God as depicted in the Bible. It looks increasingly certain that Calvin was not able to let the notion of a Trinitarian God collapse with his salvation-historical constructed realms of creation and reconciliation, which follow the time and history line of divine history embedded in the Bible.

White does not come close to Calvin's acceptance of the orthodox and scholastic notion of a Trinity; in fact, it appears as if the Trinitarian notion of God more or less totally disappeared from her works. Various of my fellow Seventh-day Adventist theologians toying with the idea of coming in line with the widely accepted doctrine of the Trinity, as accepted by the majority of churches, look at White's views as stemming, in part, from a lack of understanding of the doctrine of the Trinity, during the formative years of the Seventh-day Adventist denomination in the nineteenth century.

Some early Seventh-day Adventist leaders believed the doctrine to be unscriptural and absurd (Bates n.d., 204-205; White, J 1852, 52). The personhood of the Holy Spirit proved to be even more difficult to understand and articulate. In all her writings, White never used the term, "Trinity," although she did refer to the "three living persons of the heavenly trio" (White [1946] 1970, 615). Her comments suggest that she believed that the Scriptures taught the existence of three co-eternal divine persons (613-617). In the current debate, a large group of theologians in the Seventh-day Adventist world espouse strong Trinitarian views, which they undergird with statements from White's later writings, sayings, and doings from 1890 until her death in 1915.

What these fellow theologians do not realize is that one cannot operate with the classical view of a Trinitarian God in its most significant Latin formulation of *Deus est Trinitas*, portraying God the Father, God the Son, and God the Holy Spirit, and yet also operate with White's notion of the humanity of the Son of God blended with his divinity in continuation until the infinity of eternity as the eternal high priest in the heavenly sanctuary. Calvin, an avowed supporter of only divine persons in the Trinity—the *Deus est Trinitas* doctrine—connected the divinity of Jesus Christ, the Son of God, so closely to his humanity in his notion of an *extra-calvinisticum* that Christ's resurrected humanity currently in "heaven" stays closely connected to his divinity at the right-hand side of the Father until the infinity of eternity (Van Niekerk 2009b, 36). Later on, we will see that at some distant part of eternity, Christ, according to Calvin, will assume his original pre-incarnation status as being only divine. Calvin's whole pastoral dogmatic approach of operating with the grand acts of creation and reconciliation, albeit with lesser emphasis on God's grand acts of renewal and fulfillment at the deepest level, does not correspond with the classical doctrine of a Trinitarian God of Father, Son, and Holy Spirit.

White's hesitation to pry and inquire intrusively into the essence of God as God-self, as demonstrated in her total underemphasizing, not to say bypassing, of the doctrine of the Trinity with all its speculative elements, should be treasured by Seventh-day Adventists as part of her high respect for the range of God's grand acts, which express her view of divine history embodied and embedded in the salvation-historical trajectory of the Bible. In reflecting on God, human beings, or the natural world, White stays within the demarcated biblical historical timeline. She connects in her reflection on the Godhead "heavenly history" and "earthly history" so closely together that Christ speaks to Moses at the burning bush:

> When we approach the subject of . . . divinity . . . we may appropriately heed the words spoken by Christ to Moses at the burning bush, "Put off thy shoes from off thy feet, for the place whereon thou standest is holy ground." We must come to the study of this subject with the humility of a learner with a contrite heart (White [1953] 1985a, 348-349).

It is important that the large group of my fellow Seventh-day Adventist theologians who strongly advocate the *Deus est Trinitas*, as the view of the mature White, should be more involved in the current debate in the global theological world in which the notion of the Trinity is skeptically viewed as a fourth-century doctrinal artifact mainly devised under the influence of politicians at the ecumenical councils of the first millennium. Furthermore, while experience has demonstrated that the doctrine of the Trinity has very little impact in the lives and practical daily experience of Christians, White's emphasis on the grand acts of God as divine history embodied and embedded in the Bible should be embraced and employed as reflexive faith tools for a new way of doing concrete theology. Moreover, her reflexive coherence of faith patterning within the realms of the divine historical timeline of the Bible, especially in the first half of her life, should be opened up and extended, instead of being viewed as lacking in understanding the doctrine of the Trinity.

1.2 The Second Problem Setting: The Nature and Centrality of Christ's Reconciliation in the Array of the Grand Acts of God

One of the main challenges of this book is to describe the centrality of Christ within the range of God's acts of creation, reconciliation, renewal, and fulfillment. Calvin and White reflect on the mystery of the simultaneity of the close connection and radical difference of God, human beings, and the natural cosmic world in all the grand acts of God that is creation, reconciliation (redemption), renewal, and consummation (fulfillment). In the divine history embodied and embedded in the salvation-historical trajectory of the grand acts of God's salvation, redemption, and reconciliation in Jesus Christ, his cross, his resurrection, and intercession stand absolutely central in both Calvin's and White's view, stretching back to creation and forward to the final consummation and projected eternal bliss.

However, White contributed a slightly different view on Christ as mediator. While White does acknowledge a sequence of change of Christ's office from that of priest/mediator currently to that of *the Coming Triumphant King*, which is similar to that of Calvin's stance, more than Calvin, White depicts Christ as a perpetual mediator between divinity and humanity after the fulfilling consummation. In other words, regardless of the different phases of offices of mediator and king, which are both present in Calvin's and White's Christology (like Calvin, White does acknowledge a distinct cessation of the office of mediator), the difference is that White takes the mediating aspect of Christ throughout the ceaseless ages of eternity. Although, it must be mentioned that White does not imply that there will be a mediation of the sort that Christ is currently engaged in. She clearly states, by quoting the apostle John in Revelation 21:22 and by her further statement that there will be no more sin, that there will be no temple in the preceding life, and therefore, no veil between the redeemed people and God (White [1888] 1990a, 676-678). The difference here is embedded in White's view of the limitation that Christ has assumed by taking upon himself the human nature. To White, this perpetual retention of the human nature is a form of an everlasting mediation or a representation of humanity within the realm of divinity. This perpetual mediation makes it possible for an eternal guarantee of partnership since both parties are represented in the centrality of Christ in God's grand acts of creation, redemption, renewal, and consummation.

According to White, Christ has always been the mediator of the covenant from the past of eternity to the future of eternity (White [1953] 1985, 441). White, sticking close to the Judeo-Christian Bible in reflecting on its timeline assumingly with the mindset of Hebrews 7:1-3, portrays Christ's continued perpetual mediation after its official cessation according to the heavenly sanctuary's ministration. Once the officiating work is complete in the heavenly sanctuary, according to White, there will be no mediator for the righteous living, who will be awaiting the Second Coming of Christ. In this regard, White says:

> When he leaves the sanctuary, darkness covers the inhabitants of the earth. In that fearful time, the righteous must live in the sight of a holy God without an intercessor (White [1888] 1990a, 614).

Morris Venden, Seventh-day Adventist pastor and author, in his book, *Never Without an Intercessor* (1996, 57-69), explains what the latter statement by White means. According to Venden, there is no such a thing as the righteous ever being able to live at any time without an intercessor since the human being has always been and will always be dependent upon Christ and God. What emerges in Venden's reading of White's statement is the conspicuous clarity of the statement. White's statement in a broader context reads as follows:

> When He [Christ] leaves the sanctuary, darkness covers the inhabitants of the earth. In that fearful time, the righteous must live in the sight of a holy God without an intercessor. The restraint which has been upon the wicked is removed, and Satan has entire control of the finally impenitent. God's long-suffering has ended. The world has rejected His mercy, despised His love, and trampled upon His law. The wicked have passed the boundary of their probation; the Spirit of God, persistently resisted, has been at last withdrawn. Unsheltered by divine grace, they have no protection from the wicked one. Satan will then plunge the inhabitants of the earth into one great, final trouble. As the angels of God cease to hold in check the fierce winds of human passion, all the elements of strife will be let loose. The whole world will be involved in ruin more terrible than that which came upon Jerusalem of old . . . The same destructive power exercised by holy angels when God commands, will be exercised by evil

> angels when He permits. There are forces now ready, and only waiting the divine permission, to spread desolation everywhere (White [1888] 1990a, 614).

According to Venden (1996, 67), the above passage deals with God's intercession and intervention manifesting God's prevention of the world from collapsing into a disastrous, inhabitable dungeon of chaos. In this regard, Venden states:

> When this world no longer has an intercessor against Satan, and the four winds are let loose, all hell breaks loose. That's what it means when both the righteous and the wicked will live without an intercessor (Venden 1996, 67).

With the afore said in mind, it should therefore suffice to say that Christ's mediation, though temporarily may be deemed absent, as he will allow for the angels of destruction to do their work, will continue, since his priesthood is forever, in and after the order of Melchizedek. Hence, Christ's mediation and priesthood continues as a different phase of priesthood/mediation since there will be no temple or sanctuary, nor will there be any sin, which can be deciphered from White's emphatic suggestion of the retention of Christ's human nature into eternity:

> When God would assure us of His immutable counsel of peace, He gives His only begotten Son to become one of the human family, forever to retain His human nature as a pledge that God will fulfill His word . . . Man's substitute and surety must have man's nature, a connection with the human family whom He was to represent, and, as God's ambassador, He must partake of the divine nature, have a connection with the Infinite, in order to manifest God to the world, and be a mediator between God and man (White [1953] 1985a, 488).

This is a divergent view from Calvin, who regarded the office of mediation as transitory. Unlike White, who viewed the limitation that Christ has imposed upon himself by assuming the human nature to be perpetual and thereby rendering himself to be subservient and obsequious to God, Calvin deemed the mediation and submission of Christ to God only to be transient:

> Christ, therefore, shall reign until he appear to judge the world, inasmuch as, according to the measure of our feeble capacity, he now connects us with the Father. But when, as partakers of the heavenly glory, we shall see God as he is, then Christ, having accomplished the office of Mediator, shall cease to be the vicegerent of the Father, and will be content with the glory which he possessed before the world was . . . God will then cease to be the head of Christ, and Christ's own Godhead will then shine forth of itself, whereas it is now in a manner veiled (Calvin [1989] 2001b, 418).

It appears here that as far as Calvin is concerned, Christ's humanity, which serves to veil his divinity, will expire at some point of eternity. The reflection in this problem area revolves around the nature and the centrality of Jesus Christ in the views of Calvin and White. The reflexive discussion, on one hand, has to do with how and where does Jesus Christ's life, death, and resurrection fit into the grand acts of God's creation; God's reconciliation circumscribed in the life, death, and resurrection of Jesus Christ; God's renewal through Pentecost; and God's consummation and fulfillment of all things, culminating in the new heaven and the new earth. On the other hand, the reflexive discussion points in the direction of the nature and role of Jesus Christ in God's central act of reconciliation, redemption, and salvation.

The first dimension is thus a concentration of the discussion on the concept of the how, what, and where, and the role and function of Jesus Christ's life, death, and resurrection from beginning to end within God's grand acts as portrayed in the Bible. The second dimension deals with the question of whether we are referring to the realness of events and factual quality, and the historical and material quality of realness of the reconciliation, redemption, and salvation in Jesus Christ. The problem is how are Calvin and White perceiving Jesus Christ's humanity in being born a human to be closely connected and an equal partner to his divinity? After he had condescended into our world, what actually happened to his divinity? Did Jesus cease to be an active person in God, who is a participant in the affairs of the universe from beginning to end, while he was on earth as a human being? The other side of this question is whether he ceased to be divine at his death on the hills of Golgotha.

Both Calvin and White follow the path of the salvation-historical realness and factuality of reconciliation and salvation, embracing human beings and the natural cosmic world in the life, death, and resurrection of Jesus Christ. As a matter of necessity in being complete in what is investigated, different approaches are dealt with while one approach of *interactional substantialism* on the divinity and humanity of Christ detected in the writings of Calvin and White is treated as the main approach from which the others are measured and evaluated.

In this work, both the differences and overlapping between Calvin's and White's views are investigated. Ivan T. Blazen, writing on the Seventh-day Adventist understanding of the doctrine of salvation, said:

> Seventh-day Adventists see themselves as heirs of and builders upon the Reformation insights into biblical teaching on justification by grace through faith alone, and restorers and exponents of the fullness, clarity, and balance of the apostolic Gospel (Blazen 2000, 307).

Jesus Christ is *mysteriously divine and human* from his pre-existence, which proceeds through his life, cross, and resurrection to his post-existence. Two notions emerged in this approach that the other three approaches did not have. First, Jesus Christ mysteriously acted out his divineness sometimes and other times more his humanness in his life, death, and resurrection. Second, in a mysterious way, Jesus Christ's divinity and humanity stay together beyond the limiting notions of his pre-existence before "the virgin birth" and his post-existence on "the right hand side of the Father" in "heaven."

A first of the well-known approaches in Christianity revolves around the idea of *transformational trans-substantialism*, the humanity of Christ is sacramentally transformed by his divinity. The main Roman Catholic sacramentalist position in which Jesus Christ is seen as *the divine human being* in salvation is representative of this approach. Jesus Christ is *the divine human being*, who was the pre-existent divine Son of God, transforming the humanity of Jesus through a virgin birth into that of a sacramentalized and sacralized divine human being. This divine human being had proceeded exclusively from heaven as the divine Son of God and continues to live into his post-existence through the resurrection and the ascension in his body the Church. The limiting notion of the incarnation in this approach means that the pre-existent divine Son of God had been clothed with divinized human flesh while he was on earth. This means that the risen Son of God, who is now on the right hand side of the Father, has left behind his creaturely human flesh and is solely divine. Though this view is not propagated in current Roman Catholic theologies, it is still strongly operational in Roman Catholic ecclesial practices and sacraments from baptism to the Eucharist.

A second approach revolves around the notion of the divinity of Christ permeating his humanity, as expressed by the *consubstantialist* approach. This position has very old papers in the history of Christianity, but was given its final format by Luther and the Lutheran tradition by portraying Jesus Christ as *the human God*. This view is expounded by the majority of present-day churches in the global arena;

even a large part of Roman Catholicism and evangelicals in the Reformed/Presbyterian, Pentecostal, and charismatic worlds ascribe to the view that Christ's divinity is permeating his humanity. In alignment with this view on the scale of a permeation of the humanity by the divinity, many evangelical and pietist views operate with the idea of the divine Jesus nestled in the heart of the believer, permeating the ego-center of a human being—created by God—as the driving force of all a person's good and meaningful thoughts, acts, and doings. The great majority of Christological views found within the Evangelical Christian world embrace this view.

Jesus Christ, as *the human God* in his life, cross, and resurrection, is also the pre-existent divine Son of God who has permeated the humanity of Jesus to such an extent that he became Jesus Christ. After his resurrection, the human God is the ubiquitous divine agency that continues to permeate people's faith, the Bible, the church, and the sacraments of bread and wine.

A third approach, which is modern to the hilt, could be termed a *human-mono-substantialism*. This is mainly a liberal and humanist position that has its roots in the Renaissance of the fourteenth and fifteenth centuries and was more fully worked out in the Enlightenment period of the seventeenth to the eighteenth century. In the nineteenth to the twentieth century, this approach is circumscribed as that of a special and particular human being who, being born in a certain era of history, had a profound impact on history and functioned as one of the many important human prophets who had emerged in history. According to such a liberal and humanistic view, Jesus Christ, as a special and particular human being, is a son of God in the same way as all other human beings are sons and daughters of God.

Although there is a whole array of Catholic positions, the central Catholic *transubstantiation*, incarnation approach is one in which at conception, the human Jesus is transformed into a divine human being. This is what Catholic views of incarnation through "the virgin birth" entail. In the main

Lutheran *consubstantiation*, incarnation approach, God as the divine agency constantly permeates the human Jesus from his conception onward. This constant permeation of Jesus, the human being by his own divine character, as God's divine agency circumscribes the Lutheran view of incarnation in all other theological and ecclesial spheres. These views, as well as some forms of one-sided *interactional substantialism*, are sometimes called *anhypostatic* views, which mean that the emphasis is more on the divinity than the humanity of Christ. These views are strikingly similar to those in which the divinity is overbearingly attested in the transformed human or permeated human side. A *human-mono-substantialist* position, with its emphasis exclusively on the human Jesus and a total disregard for his divinity, seems to hold sway in a whole array of theological circles in the world today.

The main approach of this work circulates around the notion of *interactional substantialism*. In this position, the mystery of simultaneous interactional at-one-ment and at-other-ment of the divinity and humanity of Jesus Christ is embodied. The interactional inter-substantialist position has a minority status in the history of Christianity and the Christian churches. Representatives who could easily fit, albeit loosely, into this position are John Calvin, Ulrich Zwingli, and Ellen G. White. Calvin's and White's *interactional substantialist* approaches function as an evaluative tool in chapter three of this book, intersecting and comparing different approaches that emerged in history.

CHAPTER 2

God's Grand Acts as Divine History Embedded in the Bible

2.1 God's Grand Acts Open to Biblical Reflection or Speculative Theologizing?

In this chapter, what has been termed the first problem-setting revolves around the question of whether God's grand acts of creation, reconciliation, renewal, and fulfillment embodied and embedded in the divine biblical history are sufficient for our concrete reflexive activities of faith, or is there still any necessity to continue the tradition of medieval scholastics and modern speculative theology, which theologize abstractly in a realm above God's grand acts as portrayed in the divine history of the Bible?

2.1.1 Introduction

One of the widespread beliefs in the modern era amongst Christians and Christian communities is that by virtually inserting themselves into the ongoing divine history in the Old and New Testament, they experience God directly in the same way as the Israelites and the New Testament writers. This belief tells us more about the way people make sense of what the scriptural texts tell them as words from God than of the eras and contexts in which the texts have been written and composed. Were these texts written and composed by people in the usual way they tell stories of all things that happen in their lives? Or were these people inspired by God's Spirit to write these stories through their own individual sense-making experiences? Or was God's Spirit self the writer and oral composer of these stories by moving the tongue and the pen in the hand of the human speaker and writer? An overwhelming number of approaches of how people and communities make sense of the divine history told in the Bible emerged in the era since the Reformation of the sixteenth century. The majority of Christians believe that God was the direct author and player in the divine history. In the Old and the New Testament, the living God of the whole of history was and is still making history for the salvation of people in the world while simultaneously managing the whole of world history (Guthrie 1960, 3-13).

For many people in the biblical sense, God makes history and makes himself known through the timeline of divine history: starting at *creation* of everything long ago; by letting or not letting people fall into *sin;* by providing the *salvific* solution for humanity and nature in Jesus Christ; by again making history by providing the continuous *renewing* work of the Holy Spirit for people and nature; and by finally drawing people and the natural world to the end of the timeline in the *fulfillment* of the new heaven and the new earth.

Two directions were broadly taken by people and their communities who inserted themselves as partakers of the divine history into the timeline of divine history of God's grand acts of creation, reconciliation, renewal, and fulfillment in the new heaven and new earth. The first direction is that of the Roman Catholic approach; they saw themselves as a continuation of the divine history of the First Testament. That is the Old Testament for non-Catholics and the Second Testament—New Testament—for non-Catholics. They are not only a continuation from the beginning of God's act of creation, but also a total care-giving delivering of the timeline of divine history up to and after the fulfillment of the end of time. The other direction, which is propagated by the more Protestant-inclined way of making sense in the modern era, is expressed therein that the Judeo-Christian Bible from Genesis to Revelation is the total, full, and sufficient exploration area where the sense of divine salvation history couched in natural human history is readily available and obtainable in a clear sense.

The type of divine historicity observed by Calvin and White in the Old Testament and the New Testament comprises the fusion of supernatural divine acts and events with human and natural acts and events. This sort of fused divine-human-natural historicity emanates through the salvation-historical timeline of the Bible from Genesis to Revelation. According to Vos (1906, 299), the biblical timeline of supernatural historical events can be characterized as salvation-historical, soteriological, and evangelical. The extensive exposition given by Vos regarding supernatural biblical revelation as "on principle inseparable from a background of historic facts" could aptly be applied to both Calvin's and White's views (Vos 1906, 299-300). A two-level scheme of historicity is at work in the evolvement of the salvation-historical timeline in which continuous divine historical interpositions are manifested in the course of the natural evolvement of biblical history. The difference between Calvin and White regarding their approaches of a double sense of historicity, historical, and historic facts and events within the biblical timeline is not of quality, but of degree and emphasis.

Although the latter approach originates from the time of early Christianity, Calvin was one of a diverse group of sixteenth-century Reformers who finally established and affirmed the Judeo-Christian Bible as exploration area for the full and sufficient, clear and easily to be made sense of book that, according to them, depicted divine history for people's salvation in time and eternity. Though Calvin, Luther, and Zwingli were avowed advocators of the complete range of God's grand acts of creation, reconciliation, renewal, and fulfillment, they, far more than was necessary, emphasized God's grand acts of creation and reconciliation. On the other hand, White, as one of another diverse group of nineteenth-century prophetic Reformers in an era of high modernism, followed partially in the footsteps of Calvin and Luther. While giving the phenomenon of divine history expressed in the Bible, a higher concentrated and intensified quality in the nineteenth century, she simultaneously shifted the emphasis to the grand acts of reconciliation and fulfillment both revolving in and around Christ. It is significant that White's central point was Jesus Christ as present indwelling Lord and as the imminent Second Coming of Christ as God's glorious future (Damsteegt [1957] 1977, 13-16; Plantak 1998, 39).

2.1.2 Calvin's and White's Challenges

In their faith reflection throughout their writings, Calvin and White express the notion of an overarching biblical historical timeline enfolding as salvific divine history. Generally speaking, most of their works depict explicitly and implicitly the biblical denotation of God's grand acts of *creation* and *reconciliation* (redemption) through the cross and resurrection of Jesus Christ, God's wholesome *renewal* process through the Spirit of Pentecost, and God's future-directed *fulfillment* in the new heaven and new earth. They differ considerably in some areas through different ways of working in different time eras and overlap largely in other areas. One example of their considerable differences is as already stated—Calvin emphasized creation to reconciliation, while on the other hand White took a more holistic approach of: creation, reconciliation (The Cross), renewal (Pentecost) and fulfillment (Final Consummation). One commonality they shared is their emphasis on divine historicity embodied and embedded in the historical timeline of the Judeo-Christian Bible. A question has to be directed to both Calvin and White regarding the overlap they share on the biblical historical timeline as their basic area of faith reflection and guiding light of everyday experience: How can the notion of a Trinitarian God be combined with their strong emphasis on the biblically described grand acts of God as divine historical actions in which we as human beings and nature are involved?

The first challenge revolves around the radical involvement of the threesome of God, human beings, and the natural cosmic environment in each grand act of God. For many, this may seem an unnecessary challenge because it goes without saying that in each grand act of God, human beings and the natural cosmic environment are involved. However, what is of importance is that one's realm of coherent reflection of faith should not operate on two separate levels: the one ordinary and the other above the ordinary. The question is whether Calvin's and White's realms of reflection, entrenched in the divine history of the Judeo-Christian Scripture and described in the four grand acts of God, allow for a level above the divine historical series of four grand acts from where they receive biblical insights from above the ordinary?

Moreover, do Calvin, in his faith reflection on the divine historical grand acts of God in the Bible, and White, in her faith reflection on the combination of her prophetic visions and the grand acts of God in the Bible, have insight into such an extra divine realm hovering above the divine history? Calvin, with his pastorally inclined theology, vehemently opposed the construction by scholastic and speculative theology of an extra level or realm for reflection above the biblical historical timeline. Regarding the purpose of biblical history, Calvin states:

> Indeed, the principal purpose of biblical history is to teach that the Lord watches over the ways of the saints with such great diligence that they do not even stumble over a stone (Calvin [1559] 1960a, 17).

One of the questions that we attempt to answer later in this work is why Calvin accepts, on one hand, the grand acts of God, fore mostly, creation and reconciliation as his main theological realms of reflection in line with the notion of a divine biblical historical timeline? On the other hand, he contradictorily accepts the notion of a Trinitarian God of the classical literature hovering above the biblical divine historical timeline of the four grand acts of God. As a follow-up, one can also ask why, in some of Calvin's writings, the construct of a Trinity simultaneously precedes and transcends the four grand acts of God?

White, in her prophetic pastoral approach, reacted in a similar sense against the classic speculative approaches. However, what is of importance regarding her era is that she reacted also against what she viewed as the speculative scientific patterning in sciences that transcend the biblical historical timeline, which was solely set in motion and sustained by God. The best example of her emphasis on the biblical divine historical timeline is the ostensible neglect of the doctrine of the Trinity in her writings, sayings, and doings. Those in more recent Seventh-day Adventist circles, in a bid to be more readily accepted into mainline thinking regarding the Trinity, appeared to dither on the anti-speculative stance of White and early Seventh-day Adventists.

In the current debate, Whidden, regarding the early anti-speculative and anti-Trinitarian stance of White and her husband, asserts:

> While it is hard to be dogmatic about the cause/effect relationships between the healing of Adventist Arian and anti-Trinitarian expressions and soteriological imbalance, there are a number of factors that seem to come into play . . . First of all, one does not get the feeling that there was a lot of self-conscious theological reflection which transpired in any scholastic/systematic way. It appears that these developments were really quite *ad hoc*, almost to the point of seeming "providential." What is clear is that the Whites took the lead, and they mainly seemed to draw their theological cues from their pastoral concerns regarding the low estate of the perceived spiritual experience of the Seventh-day Adventist

> denomination. As they began to perceive that legalistic concerns had quite obscured the primacy of Christ as atoning sacrifice and justifying Savior, they began to reflect practically on how to bring the movement back into a greater emphasis on the centrality of Christ and His atoning sacrifice. In other words, it was practical/theological concerns, primarily having to do with an out-of-balance theology, that seemed to draw them to a more critical reflection having to do with the full deity of Christ (Whidden 1997, 6).

Early Seventh-day Adventists rejected the notion of the Trinity. The notion of the Trinity did play a somewhat undergirding role in White's reflection on the biblical historical timeline in the sense of being a divine operational tool for theological speculation of doctrinal reflection, as it did play a role in many of the mainline churches and their theologies. Karl Barth's approach of the first part of his *Church Dogmatics: The Doctrine of the Word of God, Volume 1 and 2*, is based on the notion of the Trinity centrally expressed in Jesus Christ as the revelation of God. Barth makes his salvation-historical timeline operational through an extreme concentration on Christ as the revelation of God while the notion of the Trinity increasingly plays a nearly non-existent role in the later volumes of his Church Dogmatics. While he expounds his Church Dogmatics by way of a successive description of God's acts of *creation, reconciliation, renewal, and fulfillment*, he emphasizes God's act of *reconciliation* in a reductionist sense as a Christ-centric schematization of revelation of modern day theognostic proportions.

The second challenge revolved around the question of whether the Trinitarian notion of God as Father, Son, and Holy Spirit could be respectively linked with God's acts of creation, reconciliation, renewal, and fulfillment. Even if they could be linked, God's fulfillment at the end of time has no place in the notion of a Trinitarian God. Fulfillment needs another divine person to be enacted as an act of God if the Trinitarian line of divine persons is followed. This would amount to a "quadritarian" God of Father, Son, Holy Spirit and Fulfiller. Moreover, is it still necessary to speak of a Trinity hovering above the biblical depiction of God's grand acts of creation, reconciliation, renewal, and fulfillment? By accepting and supporting the doctrine of the Trinity, Calvin did not follow his main approach of strictly reflecting within the realm of the biblically portrayed grand acts of God. Although he mostly emphasized creation and reconciliation as the realms of his reflexive activities, he constantly in the most practical of practical experiences engaged God, human beings, and nature as his real Trinitarian partners of his everyday reflection of faith. The question why Calvin, in his strong emphasis on the reflection realms of creation and reconciliation, added the notion of a Trinitarian God that hovers above history is difficult to understand.

White, on the other hand, lived in the nineteenth century world where the sense-making experience of the notion of the Trinity had already been experienced as something far away from the salvific timeline of biblical history. The question for followers of White of whether she denied or fully embraced the notion of the Trinity is not of a real historical and contextual nature. The notion of the Trinity to a large extent is not White's main operational hypothesis. Her emphasis on the divine historical timeline of the Bible from Genesis to Revelation made the doctrine of the Trinity redundant in her writings. White and other Seventh-day Adventist members who totally underemphasized the notion of a Trinitarian God—some even rejected the Trinity—were closer to the biblical historical timeline than the majority of mainline churches who confessed the notion of a Trinity that in any case has played a tiny role in the daily experiences of their members.

The third challenge of Calvin and White has to do with the question whether they lay equal emphasis on all four of God's grand acts of creation, reconciliation, renewal, and fulfillment as enactment of the biblical historical timeline. In Calvin's way of doing, it seems as if his reflection gives more weight to God's acts of creation and reconciliation. His whole approach thereby obtains a strong leaning toward the past. One has to admit that Calvin's view of reconciliation (redemption) was to such extent extended that it embraced the experience of Calvin's present situation through the linkage with the Holy Spirit as the divine renewing renovator of everything. Calvin's view of reconciliation extends into eternity through Christ as the perpetual mediator, thereby interceding between God and human beings and continuing into the future fulfillment to such an extent that the full spectrum of God's grand acts is fully maintained. As Calvin's reflection was primarily directed at God's grand acts of creation and redemption, God's thought and will, pre-existing before creation, could only be read from creation—before and after the fall—and by which God determined through his will the structures of creation.

Adam and Eve, to a large extent viewed as historical figures by Calvin, receive in this scheme a before and after treatment—in paradise before falling into sin and especially after falling into sin—which emerged as the determining factor causing the total depravity of all human beings. Every part of the biblical history is directed to the reconciliation in Christ as the mirror through which the determination procedures comes to light in people's lives. The main question was "How am I saved and who is saving me?" Thus, a person was asking whether he or she was saved by the Church with all its rituals or by God through Christ and endorsed by the Word of God. In this, the Judeo-Christian Bible became an authoritative divine source and book of history, presenting people with enough to know for this life and eternity. The Bible has become the exploration and source book that actually and virtually expresses God's historical events as divine truths, which the Reformers such as Calvin reflected up on as the light and guidance for their lives.

Regarding White in the section on the historical background earlier, the point is made that the mainline Protestant world of the era before the nineteenth century placed the emphasis mainly on two of the foursome of God's grand acts, namely that of creation and reconciliation, underemphasizing renewal and God's future directed fulfillment acts. In the early part of the nineteenth century, the pendulum swung to the last two grand acts of God: renewal through the Spirit and the future fulfillment of everything in the new heaven and the new earth. It is only with the continuation and perpetual role of Christ's investigative judgment in the holy sanctuary that the continuation with the creation filled past is fully maintained.

The main question was: "First, what happens to me in the afterlife after I have died?" Second: "What happens to me before and after the Second Coming of Christ?" In this, the Judeo-Christian Bible became a history book in a special divine sense specifically because of the emerging features of inerrancy and infallibility it gradually attained in many of the groups in this era. The Bible has become the source and exploration book that actually and virtually expresses God's historical events as divine truths mirrored in society and science. A view is only to be accepted and appropriated by them—that is, if a society is a God-fearing society and a science is an actual real science looking for God's truth in creation, reconciliation, renewal and fulfillment.

The third challenge is trickier than the earlier two because it is in the nature of traditions and their followers that they would claim to advocate and propagate the most biblical, truthful, and balanced position of all for their main ancestor and for their own position among those who are earnestly engaged in concrete biblical reflection. Therefore, to ask the question to what extent are the four grand acts of God emphasized on a par and with equal weight in the work and writings of Calvin and White may seem grossly unfair to both their followers. We are portraying their respective emphasis. Trying to detect whether Calvin or White could be termed more biblical, is not our focus. Our aim is to describe as many of their logical intricacies as possible in the eras in which they lived.

2.2 Dialectics, Scholastics, and Speculative Theology

2.2.1 Scholastic and Speculative Theology

Calvin and White, having been described in the past as not theologians in the real sense of the word, consistently defied the temptation to operate with three separate avenues for God, human beings, and the natural cosmic world. Instead, they gave more satisfactorily expression of the mystery of the simultaneous connection and differentiation of God, human beings, and the natural cosmic environment through their works.

In many instances, the theological and philosophical investigation and speculation on God, human beings, and nature was formalized into highly abstract speculative works such as that of the medieval scholastics. When such speculative constructs entered the space of the church or church communities after the necessary struggle between protagonists of different schools, these scholastic constructs acquired the status of ecclesial and divinely sanctioned doctrines, only to be slavishly accepted by followers.

Calvin and White, on the other hand, also seemed to have overcome the classic procedure of rigidly setting God, human beings, and the natural cosmic world apart with the main aim of speculating and reflecting in a bifocal way on the essence of either God or human beings or the natural world. The typical essence-seeking procedure of medieval scholastics and current neo-orthodox schools of theology investigate the essence of God, a human being, or the natural world without the intermediary role of the events and processes of history and the doings and actions of human beings.

Calvin and White have largely overcome the simultaneous strong scholastic separation of a bifocal nature of God, human beings, and the natural world. They, however, portray a dialectic of some sort between God's transcendence and God's immanence, Godly and humanly/worldly affairs, divine history of the biblical timeline and world history in general, and eternal and finite levels of making sense.

The speculative treatment of God, human beings, and the natural cosmic world is aligned with the typical approach of the medieval scholastics of vigorously and speculatively investigating the essence of God as "God is in God-self" in separation from God as "God is for us." God's power, for instance, solely discussed as the notion of "God as God in himself" is regarded by Calvin as the naked absolute power of God, which he viewed as tyranny (Oberman 1991, 17).

The intention here is not to go into an investigation of dialectics, as one type of argumentation with its concomitant branch of logic, in which this type of argumentation is discussed in contradistinction with the scientific and rhetorical types, as portrayed in Aristotle's works, *Topica and De Sophisticicis Elenchis* (1928). The background of types of dialectical schemes of the relationship of God and human beings, divine history, and world history; God's transcendence and God's immanence; the finite containing the infinite and the finite not containing the infinite; and between divine history demarcating human and world history and divine history intervening in human and world history are touched upon. Different trajectories of medieval scholastics as well as nominalism are described, leading to dialectical views of Calvin's sixteenth century and the nineteenth century where Hegel and White's types of dialectical approaches are discussed.

2.2.1.1 Neo-Platonic Scholastics of the Fifth to the Eleventh Century

In the early scholastics, in which Augustine's neo-platonic views held sway, dialectics were viewed in the platonic sense, as essentially dialogical in nature. On one hand, in the dialogical to and fro encounter of one mind (*logos*) with another (*logos*), the vertical intuitive knowledge of the truth of the real and immutable world is intuited and contemplated as wisdom or sage knowledge. Wisdom or sage knowledge is made up of shadowy reflexes or vague embodiments of the real world within the interlocution of the two minds. On the other hand, the concrete, changeable, and ever-shifting knowledge refers to the external senses of the two *logoi* or minds (Torrance 1988, 27-28).

To Plato, the weight is on the intuitive and contemplative truths of the eternal and real world with less weight on the unreal ordinary world of the senses. It is understandable when God is brought into this dualistic scheme by the early scholastics that the intuitive attention was only directed to the essence of the immutable and abstract God. Intuitive seeing with the inner eye of the mind is more important with regard to the divine truth and God-self than the outer eyes of the senses, which are directed toward impressions on the senses from the world of fleeing phenomena or appearances. The question of the quality of reality of the outer world of appearances nearly always haunted followers of Plato. Is the latter world directed to the senses then, real or unreal, semi-real or semi-unreal? The closer the real and unreal worlds are a splitting or mirrored image of each other, the less there is a difference between the two.

With the early scholastics, the essence of God was mirrored into the mental world of the contemplating and speculating human being. In the Augustinian tradition, the main emphasis is on the mirrored, revealed image of God's essence as the main factor of mediation. In the neo-platonic tradition, a similar speculative investigative treatment was dished out to human beings and the natural world, whereby "a human being's soul" is speculatively investigated as main inner substance in separation from "a human being's body" as a lesser outer substance directed to other human beings and the natural world. The natural environment was speculatively divided into a noumenal substance and phenomenal appearance side. Access into the noumenal, the substance side of natural things, could only happen through intellectual intuition devoid of the outer phenomenal and appearance side of things.

The main line of reflection in the platonic and neo-platonic schemes is that of an imaging and mirroring procedure between "God in God-self" and "God directed to us." The procedure is in a similar sense employed in a mirroring and reflective sense between God and human beings and God and the natural world.

2.2.1.2 Aristotelean Scholastics of the Eleventh to the Thirteenth Century

In later scholastics—actually termed the early scholastics in the literature of the eleventh to the thirteenth century—the narrative changed because of the impact and influence of the philosophy of Aristotle, in which the emphasis of the processual character of mediation largely replaced the notion of reflected and mirrored images of the essence of God. Aristotle, deviating from Plato, set the relationship between the dome of the mind of theoretical (contemplative) knowledge and the horizontal dome of the mind of sensible knowledge as a unitary processual scheme. This means that the "ideas" or objects of our theoretical contemplative notions do not exist apart from, but are embodied and embedded in the concrete, individual data of the dome of the sensible world. It is one and the same reality that reveals itself under an abstract, universal, static aspect to the theoretical intellect and under a concrete, manifold, dynamic aspect to the senses. What is of importance is that the processual character of the relationship between the theoretical intellect and sensible experience moves to and fro, and the one is not suppressed by the other, as is the temptation in various platonic schemes.

The Christian theologians and philosophers of the late Middle Ages, especially Thomas Aquinas, took up the emphasis of the Aristotelean processual relationship of the to and fro movement between theoretical knowledge and sensible knowledge with a whole array of distinctions between primary and secondary causes, making it one of the cardinal doctrines of scholastic theology and philosophy, thereby giving birth to the doctrine of modern realism. The approach of moderate realism taught in conjunction with Aristotle, the notion of *universalia in rebus*—that is, the generic concepts—are built into the individual entities and appear through viewing of the individual entities in the human mind. When the emphasis was directed to the extreme end of the top of the ladder where the primary causes had been effectuated, the emphasis of reflection was necessarily directed to God in a highly speculative theological mode.

The main line of reflection in the Aristotelean and neo-Aristotelean processes is that of a processual procedure between "God in God-self" and "God directed to us" expressed in various speculative processes, starting in God-self in whom as an absolute thinking mind the primary and first causes of everything else toward us as human beings are housed.

2.2.1.3 Nominalism and the Scholastics of the Eleventh to the Sixteenth Century

In the era since the eleventh century, a struggle emerged around the universal and particular character of concepts, words, beliefs, and things. The struggle was termed "the struggle of the universals." Only in the sixteenth century did the struggle of "realists" and "nominalists" recede without resulting in a satisfactory solution.

The realists of the middle ages viewed the universals (*universalia*) as things (*res*), cases, or instances that have the quality of realness. They really exist. We have to take into account that in this scheme, an increase in the degree of realness depends on an increase in the degree of generality and universality. The correlation between increasing degrees of generality and increasing levels of realness can best be illustrated with the neo-platonic metaphysics: The closer things are to God, the more realness of being they have as God, the Absolute, is simultaneously the most real (*ens realissimum*). Anselm's ontological proof for the existence of God rests on this assumption that the Absolute one, which is simultaneously the most Perfect one (*ens perfectissimum*), could only be thought to exist in thinking (Heussi 1971, 201).

Thus, God's existence flows from God's conceptuality or logicality. Extreme realism taught, closely following Plato, *universalia ante res*—universal or general concepts are extremely real and exist in their realness before the individual things. Moderate realism in alignment with Aristotle taught *universalia in rebus*—universal and general concepts lie in the individual things and enter through observance of the individual things in the human mind (Heussi 1971, 200-201).

Nominalists taught the notion of *universalia post res*. This means that universal and general concepts are plain abstract segments, terms, or words (*nomina*) of the human rational mind regarding individual singular things as the only truthful real things. The nominalists turned the whole scheme of the ladder, of which each step to the top is an ascending step of increasing realness to the most real being God, around and compressed all of reality and realness onto the level of the first step of the ladder of the individual things.

Nominalists had been called all sorts of names from atheists to secularists, from illusionists to non-realists. However, against all schemes that tend to set nominalism against realism as the real realists, a new realism was born that did not fit the sensible framework of the classic extreme and moderate realist positions. This new view of what is reality, real, and realism emerged in the ambience of the *via moderna*, which included the era of the Renaissance humanists, and the *devotio moderna* and nominalism was intrinsically part of the new realism.

The most known representative of the earlier nominalist movement was Roscellinus of Compiegne in the eleventh century, who, in applying nominalism to the doctrine of the

Trinity, came to a denial of the unity of being of the three persons of the Trinity. According to his contemporaries, Roscellinus landed in tritheism (three Gods). Since the synod of Soisson 1092 CE, where Roscellinus' views were condemned, nominalism was held as heresy (Heussi 1971, 201). According to Heussi, since the 1100s, realism was the accepted view by a minority in its extreme, platonic form and by the majority in a moderate Aristotelian form (1971, 201).

Heiko A. Oberman, writing about the era of the fifteenth to the sixteenth century on nominalism or *via moderna*, states:

> The ideas of the *via moderna* are on a wide scale absorbed by non-Franciscans, infiltrating even the doctrinally well-disciplined Dominican order and shaping the piety of thousands of sermons preached all over Europe—a source still largely untapped by scholarship. In the second place, nominalism proves to be the more comprehensive category, as the movement that not only survived, but even flourished long after Ockham and Ockhamism were condemned by the University of Paris in September 1339, and again in December 1340 (Oberman 1986, 26).

Oberman's comprehensive research on the Middle Ages, the Renaissance, and the Reformation of the sixteenth century portrays a far more complex, interesting, and interlinked background of these eras than has thus far been delivered by various traditional theologians, philosophers, and historians on these eras. His thesis that nominalist ideas reflect simultaneously the spirit of the times in a search for new securities while acting as a real (co-) agent in bringing forth these new ideas of the modern way (*via moderna*) and as the onset of modern ways of experience, delivered various meaningful results. The sensible change from the old way of experience to the new way of experience is to be seen as that of nominalists cutting higher and increasing levels of realness to the top, in the "vertical" sense of the word, by insisting and compressing all realness and full reality of our experienced world into and onto the lower steps of the ladder, in a more "horizontal" realm.

In today's terms, one would say that nominalism would have received consistent bad press while it was actually the harbinger of the modern era. A few elements have to be taken into account. The well-known insistence of nominalists on God's *potentia ordinata*—God's power as God has ordered and still ordering all things to existence—might seem as if God's freedom was limited. However, a counter-view of the nominalist point of view is that God could have decreed—*de potentia absoluta*—through God's absolute power to create another world, to choose other means of salvation, and to establish another order. But God has committed himself to this world, to the Church, and the order as we know it.

What happened in this changeover from the old to the new mindset is that this distinction of nominalists of God's ordering and God's absolute power is a continuous reminder that the reality and the world we live in is contingent and full of incidental occurrences and individual things that are the result of a divine decree, a contract, and covenant of God (*pactum Dei*) (Oberman 1986, 27). The world and our reality is not set as a continuous cascading vertical down-flowing process from God's being to the most individual event and thing or a continuous mirroring and reflection of God's being in the most individual event and thing in our world.

What nominalists did was to level a protest against the scheme of ascending realness from lesser realness in the natural world to God as the most real of all. They devised a scheme that embraces and encapsulates the realness and reality of God, human beings, and the natural world, not a scheme in which the quality of realness and reality we live in was hierarchically constructed.

Oberman says in regard to the notion of realness, reality, and realism as central to the nominalist program:

> Hunger for reality is so much the mark of nominalism that it is perhaps humorous but certainly a misleading

> tradition that bequeathed upon its opponents the name "realists." What is often called Ockham's razor is the slashing away of the hierarchy of being, of ideas, and concepts, which sheer speculation had invented (Oberman 1986, 27).

One can understand that in the era of the fourteenth to the sixteenth century, this created uncertainty and anxiety as to how and where the boundaries between God, human beings, and the natural world are to be set. Bouwsma describes Calvin's ambivalence regarding boundaries and margins as follows:

> Calvin's anxiety also operated at deeper levels. It found radical expression in his ambivalence about the order of nature. He clung, at times with frantic tenacity, to the conception of a natural order that had traditionally helped human beings to feel comfortable in the world. But this conception was also antithetical to his deep sense of the incomprehensibility of God and the contingency of the world (Bouwsma 1988, 33).

Nominalists clearly distinguished God from human beings and the natural world, but in their scheme, they clearly let God, human beings, and the natural world appear within the same framework of realness and reality.

Though Calvin reacted against the nominalist sweeping logic that cut away and slashed the upper level of speculative theology of the earlier scholastics, he made use of the nominalist scheme as the basic scheme of his *Institutes* of 1559, in which God's creation and reconciliation as portrayed in biblical history are construed as reflexive realms in which divine and human history are reflexively enacted and are thus to be followed and applied in people's lives (Van Niekerk 2009b, 33f).

Another reaction and protest of nominalists was against what they regarded as "wild speculation" and "vain curiosity" of the scholastics operating mainly in terms of Aristotle's philosophy. Their reaction against the scholastics of neo-Aristotelean branding was directed at the vertical cascading triadic scheme or movement from the top. In that branding, God was allotted a logical divine mind full of possibilities—the so-called *ens perfectissimum* of Anselm; human beings in an analogical sense have a logical mind filled, in a lesser sense than God, with possibilities; and the natural world at the lowest end has a "logical mind" least filled with possibilities, not to say devoid of possibilities (Heussi 1971, 201).

The reaction of nominalism as expressive of the *via moderna* went in the direction of the sternest opposition to the claims of logicality, intellect, and reason when these are not verified by the tests of the new scheme of embracing experience of God, human beings, and the natural world. Nominalists were careful not to construct causal relations cascading from God as the primal and first causes to the level of secondary causes where human beings and the natural world operated in the older scholastic scheme (Oberman 1986, 28). In this way, the chain of causation is reduced to observable second causes, a major advance in the transition from *the* speculative law of nature to the observable *laws* of nature (Oberman 1986, 28).

In a general way, Oberman states:

> The underlying intention of nominalism is best described in terms of the late medieval revolution against the meta-categories that obfuscate reality. Just as it rejected metaphysics to establish physics, so nominalism ventured to strip theology of her distorting meta-theological shackles, with the result that the Scriptures and the prior decrees of God were emphasized at the expense of natural theology (Oberman 1986, 28).

In conclusion, one has to recall that the scholastic and speculative approaches operated on the basis of three cascading levels of God, human beings, and the natural world, each level expressing a difference in the quality of realness or logicality. Human beings and the natural world were linked to the most real or the most filled of logical possibilities—God at the top end of the hierarchical scale. The whole scheme is brought into operation by a revelational mirroring or revelational processual cascading scheme in the movement: God → human beings → natural world. In the modern era from the sixteenth century onward, the three avenues revolving respectively around God, human beings, and the natural environment are still underlying the broad avenues housing the religious-theological disciplines, human sciences, and natural sciences. The three complex bundles of disciplines and sciences, though divided and sometimes set in a struggle with each other, existed alongside each other for many centuries at modern universities. In the practicalities of modern universities, through shifts and turns, one of the three avenues usually receives a higher rating up to the point of denying or rejecting the claims of one or both of the other avenues.

Oberman points as an overall conclusion to the emerging new image of God implied in the emphasis of nominalism on God's *potentia ordinata*, God's power in his ordered and continuous ordering of ordinances:

> God is a covenant God; his *pactum* or *foedus* is his self-commitment to become the contractual partner in creation and salvation. Here originates the Pelagianism of the *facere quod in se est*, which stands in the area of justification for the meager but sufficient human moral efforts which God has contracted, accepted or pledged to reward. In this emphasis on covenantal and not necessary relationships between God and his world as well as between God and his Church, man is no longer primarily a second cause moved by the prime mover and first cause. In the nominalist view, man has become the appointed representative and partner of God, responsible for his own life, society, and world, on the basis and within

> the limits of the treaty or *pactum* stipulated by God (Oberman 1986, 29).

The carrier notion of the nominalist program is the notion of contingency and contingent, meaning the reality and the world we live in is full of incidental occurrences and individual things. In the nominalist program, this should be understood in two directions, embracing both the vertical relation, God-human-world, and the horizontal relation, past-world-human-future. Reality and the world, which is full of incidental occurrences and individual things happening and set within the ordered framework of God's power, should not be seen as unreliable and unrelated accidental occurrences and things. In the vertical dimension of God-human-world in nominalism, Godly factors are Godly factors; human factors are human factors; and natural worldly factors are natural worldly factors. In the horizontal dimension of past-world-human-future, an alternate form of contingent and contingency opens up a complexity of human and natural worldly factors, added to divine factors in the course of events viewed in the past or toward the future.

2.2.2 Calvin's Double-Sided Dialectic

Calvin shared with the humanist Renaissance scholars of his day a strong reaction against early and late medieval scholasticism, especially with regard to its speculative contemplations and extremities of speculative essence-seeking and inquiring about the substances of God, human beings, and the natural world. Calvin simultaneously reacted vehemently and aligned himself with scholastic types of the thirteenth century such as that of Thomas Aquinas and fourteenth-century scholastics of the Duns Scotus and Ockham type, which had been given the name of nominalism (Oberman 1986, 253-258).

The reaction against the scholastics among Renaissance humanists to whom Calvin initially belonged was so strong that it is sometimes difficult to understand Calvin's mindset as he sometimes rejects and sometimes embraces notions and views from the same group of persons.

Vives, operating within the Renaissance humanist circles, states about scholastic dialecticians:

> [They] have invented for themselves certain meanings of words contrary to all civilized custom and usage, so that they may seem to have won their argument when they are not understood . . . For when they are understood, it is apparent to everyone that nothing could be more pointless, nothing more irrational. So, when their opponent has been confused by strange and unusual meanings and word-order, by wondrous suppositions, wondrous ampliations, restrictions, appellations, they then decree for themselves, with no public decision or [verdict] a triumph over an adversary not conquered but confused by new feats of verbal legerdemain (Vives 1979, 57-59).

Calvin's dislike was conceived during his studies in Sorbonne and remained so intense throughout his life that he could hardly refrain from indulging in a strongly emotive denunciation of the sophistry produced by the scholastics and the nominalist views of the theologians of Sorbonne. Calvin reacted against the Renaissance humanists in his later years, but took much from their way of doing into his writings. Calvin reacted vehemently against medieval scholasticism, especially against nominalism, whether in its terminist dialectics and logical hair-splitting or in their stress on the free will of God and human beings as well as all their speculative views on the combination of merit and free will. His reaction was especially against the notion of merit, supposedly built into human beings in a primordial sense and widespread speculative reflection on the notion of a free will as part of the human condition and constitution (Torrance 1988, 73). Nevertheless, Calvin owed much to his medieval inheritance, even in his own work where he changed what he learned. In many instances, Calvin adapted schemes from the various forms of scholastics and Renaissance humanist schools into his Calvinian sense-making theological-philosophical scheme.

The logic of dialectics, as used in Scholasticism, was directed at abstract issues and abstract concepts. The scholastic approach of an encounter of two abstract ideas, words, or notions has been replaced with a person-directed dialog revolving around the notion of consciousness between two minds within the triadic framework of seeing, saying, and hearing, which emerged from the writings of Renaissance humanists and John Mair, who was well versed in the thought patterns of nominalism (Torrance 1988, 28, 88-89).

Partially differing and partially aligning himself with the scholastics of the late Middle Ages and nominalism and Renaissance humanism, Calvin's dialectic is rolled out as an encounter between "mind and mind," that is between God's mind and human minds and between the time dimensions of the past, the present as the natural world and human beings, and the future.

Ganoczy makes the following statement about the two kinds of dialectic in Calvin's writings:

> Anyone who reads Calvin's work is struck by a tension that characterizes not only the method but also the substance of his theology. It is as if there are two kinds of dialectic. The first is the art of reasoning according to the demands of formal logic, which gives great clarity and strength to statements; the second is a habit of systematically placing the divine and the human elements in opposition to each other and then resolving the tension with the help of a principle that synthesizes the opposites (Ganoczy 1987, 185).

Ganoczy is correct regarding the second kind of dialectic in which Calvin systematically places the divine and the human elements in opposition to each other and then resolves the tension with the help of a principle that synthesizes the opposites. Calvin's dialectic between God's acts of creation and redemption, which Calvin acquired through his heavily involved and engaged biblical epistemology, is not emphasized by Ganoczy. Van Niekerk, on the other hand, points to the double sidedness of Calvin's God-human-world approach:

> Calvin's sense-making approach, which is embedded in his *Institutes of the Christian Religion* (1559), can be construed as a story embodying two reflexive realms, one of creation and the other of redemption. In each of these realms, two trajectories operate closely together. The first is a "vertical" mirroring trajectory with God and human beings facing each other. The second is a "horizontal" trajectory consisting in a process that begins with God approaching human beings and the natural cosmic world (Van Niekerk 2009b, 33).

However, Ganozcy is correct that in Calvin's way of working with the triad of God, human beings, and the natural cosmic world, the natural created world plays a slightly lesser role than God and human beings. He suggested that because of the influence of Stoicism on Calvin, the natural cosmic world, in comparison to the weight given to the pointers of God and humanity, is degraded (Ganoczy and Scheld 1982, 46, 49). On the other hand, he relativized the links between Stoicism and Calvin by making use of a typical Calvinistic theologistic strategy by stating that Calvin's grounding in the biblical-Christian faith softens any similarity with Stoicism and should not be taken totally serious (Ganozcy and Scheld 1982, 52). The main reason why the natural created world is a bit less emphasized is to be found in the one leg of Calvin's "vertical" mirroring trajectory in which God and human beings are facing each other while neglecting the natural cosmic world as an initiating agency partner in the triad of God, human beings, and the natural cosmic world.

Calvin's treatment of Christ, the Church, faith as experiential dimension, and the sacraments all reflected on within the "vertical" mirroring trajectory in which God and human beings, facing each other, portray the same divine and human contracted and concentrated duality. According to van Niekerk, the particular contracted and concentrated divine/human duality expresses "an inter-substantial intense closeness and radical difference. There is no trans-substantial transforming of the human by the divine or con-substantial permeation of the human by the divine or the divine by the human in Calvin's view of a dual particularity of the contracted and concentrated divinity and humanity of Christ" (Van Niekerk 2009b, 44).

Charles Partee, while admitting that a dialectic in the broad sense of the word plays a role in Calvin's work, directs his main attention solely to the unity of Christ as basic point of departure:

Admittedly, one can find in Calvin a dialectic of ideal and real, universal and hypothetical, necessary and contingent, rhetoric and philosophic, freedom and predestination, divine and human perspectives, justification and sanctification, and so on. However, valorizing the dialectic process in this way overstates the situation. More basic to Calvin's theology is the unity of truth revealed in Jesus Christ (Partee 2008, 38).

Calvin describes Christ dually in the divine and human sense, "as God he is the destination to which we move; as man, the path by which we go. Both are found in Christ alone" (Calvin [1559] 1960c, 2).

In Calvin's words, between Christ as God, our destination, and us, the trajectory is anagogical and mirroring as a sort of step-by-step seeing and hearing of the Word. Between Christ as a human being, our path, and us as human beings, the trajectory is analogical and processual as ongoing understanding. Regarding the triad of seeing, hearing, and saying, the scholastics underemphasized the hearing and saying as personal encounter between God and human beings and between human beings themselves. The seeing of God and human beings was strongly couched in the language of neo-platonic intuitive mirroring best expressed by the idea of the beatific vision that a child of God will have when God will be all in all. Calvin learned from Major and Luther that intuitive seeing sprouting mainly from neo-platonic schemes and Aristotelian processual links between saying and hearing could be collapsed into a single scheme (Torrance 1988, 88-89).

2.2.3 Hegelian Dialectic

In the nineteenth century, the German philosopher G.F.W. Hegel worked out a theoretical historical scheme in which he demonstrates Kant's idea in his *Critique of Pure Reason* (2003) of dialectical reasoning leading to contradictions as a correct assumption. He, however, rejected Kant's view that when general logic as a dialectical logic is seen as an embracing system of logic, it amounts to logic of illusion. For Hegel, the contradictions of the Kantian view of dialectic became the true form of the history and the historical processes in the world of human beings. Hegel's conception of dialectic could be viewed as an "ongoing dialectical see-sawing movement of the Truth expressing itself as Spirit," or the way the absolute mind or spirit is unfolding itself repetitively as the truth in the historical processes in an ongoing dialectical see-sawing movement in which human beings and the natural environment are taken up. Hegel's method involved the grasping of "opposites in their unity, the positive in the negative."

Hegel expresses the different aspects of the ongoing dialectical movement in the first edition of his *Encyclopedia of Philosophy* as follows:

> There are three aspects in every thought which is logically real or true: the abstract or rational form, which says what something is; the dialectical negation, which says what something is not; the

> speculative-concrete comprehension: A is also that which it is not, A is not non-A. These three aspects do not constitute three parts of logic, but are moments of everything that is logically real or true. They belong to every philosophical concept. Every concept is rational, is abstractly opposed to another, and is united in comprehension together with its opposites. This is the definition of dialectic (Hegel 1959, 82).

The whole process of truth rolling out in history develops through the medium of contradiction. In the unfolding of the historical processes as a whole, Hegel's theory of dialectic plays a central role. The word dialectic stems from the Greek word *dialegein*, meaning to dialogue, discourse, or argue. Though Hegel did not actually use the terms of the triad thesis, antithesis, and synthesis in the same context, his dialectic is generally regarded as a process of argument proceeding by triads, each triad consisting of thesis, antithesis, and synthesis. One starts with an initial proposition, the thesis; this proves to be inadequate and generates its opposite antithesis. This in turn proves inadequate, and the opposites are taken up into a synthesis. Hegel calls the synthesis a sublation (*Aufhebung*) of thesis and antithesis—that is, it preserves what is rational in them, but cancels what is irrational.

The whole triadic process is repeated in Hegel's writings, sayings, and doings in different contexts, but always concludes in a synthesis that is at the same time a new thesis generating its opposite, the antithesis, and so on. An important contribution to the nineteenth century is Hegel's view that in these triadic processes there are leaps, thereby rejecting the popular traditional doctrine of his era that "nature makes no leaps." To Hegel the latter doctrine is clearly false; there are many cases (for example the transformation of water into steam or ice) in which a new state does not appear gradually but appears as a leap (Flew and Priest 2002, 160).

In the first part of the nineteenth century, the notion of the Divine or Absolute mind manifesting itself in historical processes directed to the future in leaps played itself out in European societies and the Americas in a widespread sense-making logic competing with the notion of evolutionism as another approach. While Hegel employed the notion of leaps and Marx made use of the idea of abrupt revolutionary changes as answer to the ongoing processes in history, Lamarck's (d.1829) evolutionary theory of the inheritance of acquired characters and Darwin's (d.1892) evolutionary theory of different species brought about by natural selection described evolutionary processes as slow and gradual changes over successive generations (Hale, Saunders and Margham 2005, 147).

Since the early part of the nineteenth century, many views of Christ emerged in which the Absolute mind or Spirit emanates from above as a divine evolutionary rolling out into history, simultaneously embracing the whole of humanity and the natural cosmic world. What is of importance here is that the spiritual divine component manifests itself intrinsically in the materiality of the world. The latter view of the Godhead rolling out into humanity in an evolutionary sense was widely accepted in the nineteenth century in the European and the American world. Reference is often made to the statement of F. C. Oetinger that corporeality is the end of all the ways of God (Barth [1932] 1975, 134). In the nineteenth century world, the approach carried by the statement that corporeality is the end of the ways of God had been directly applied in the Christological sense to Christ, or to the consciousness of human beings in general.

2.2.4 White's Dialectic

In the nineteenth-century Christian world, including the whole variety of churches, the close linkage and connection of God to historical processes could be seen in a closer binding and connection of divine history in the Bible and the biblical timeline expressed in the Bible. In this era, the idea that the Bible is inerrant and infallible—coming to its acme in the 1920s in the United States—was already strongly on track among Christians (Harris 1998, 19-56). On the basis of the same logic by which Hegelians constructed the whole of history as the sphere outside the biblical timeline where God as the divine mind synthesized himself through a dialectical see-sawing process with the human mind, many Christians awaiting the imminent Second Coming of Christ as introduction to the end of times in the nineteenth century employed the notion of a dialectical divine history, enacted between God and human beings and divinely set by God in successive dispensations of the biblical timeline.

Increasingly in the nineteenth century, a dialectical divine/human historical ambience embodied in respective divinely ordained dispensational biblical eras from Genesis to Revelation took root in the experiential worlds of many people in North America. These dispensations are not only portrayed in the Bible as something happening on the surface of the Bible, but could be regarded as intrinsically part of the materiality of the divine historical textuality of the Bible. Moreover, the dialectically divine/human history set in dispensational biblical eras became increasingly the divine template as sort of an experience for the rest of world history. A second dialectic appears between divine biblical history in dispensations and world history in the sense of sacred divine history and worldly history. In the sixteenth century world of Calvin, the relationship between biblical history and world history had been set as the relationship of "particular" and "general" history in which God is simultaneously at work through his Spirit, albeit in a particular and general way.

Two intersecting tendencies that played a major role in a large part of the Christian world in the nineteenth century are portrayed in White's writings, sayings, and doings. The *first trajectory* of White's faith reflexive pattern is the centrality of Christ in the duality of God and human beings facing each other in a closely connected, concentrated, and contracted dialectical way. In Christ emerges the divine/

human template of how God is connectively working with his creation throughout God's history with human beings. White portrays God and human beings as directly involved in the matters terrestrial and celestial in Christ. White states:

> In Christ, the family of earth and the family of heaven are bound together. Christ glorified is our brother. Heaven is enshrined in humanity, and humanity is enfolded in the bosom of Infinite Love (White [1898] 1948a, 25-26).

The sentence about humanity points to the central theme in White's writings of God's communicative love manifested through and in Christ. The theme of God's wrath, which had been raised by some Adventists as becoming deemphasized when the love of God is too strongly emphasized, could be met in the following way: God's wrath and anger toward sinners and his destruction of them (Isaiah 28:21), as manifested in the biblical historical dynamics, could only be viewed as contradictory and incompatible with his continuous communicative love from a static mindset. This isolates the many references to God's wrath in the Bible from the dynamics of God's communicative love.

The main problem with these isolated mirrored readings is that they are presented with divine authority in their isolation. The wrath and anger of God in White's works is continuously subsumed in the dynamics of God's manifested dynamic love. By accepting the will of God—God's law and forgiveness offered through free grace to all in Jesus Christ—the wrath of God is deflected. More than that is speculative. In White's writings, the paradigmatic divine/human coming together of God's infinite love through and in Christ permeates from the middle of history, in a retrocipatory way; in God's actions through the establishment of the Ten Commandments to the dateless ages before creation; and in an anticipatory way, through the sanctuary ministry to the eternal era after God's fulfillment and consummation.

According to White, Christ took our nature and dwelled among us, thereby expressing the dialectic between heaven and earth, divinity and humanity, from above in the sense that:

> Divinity was revealed in humanity; the invisible glory in the visible human form. Men could learn of the unknown through the known; heavenly things were revealed through the earthly; God was made manifest in the likeness of men. So it was in Christ's teaching: the unknown was illustrated by the known; divine truths by earthly things with which the people were most familiar (White [1900] 1941, 17).

White, in her view of incarnation, is not operating with an impersonal, cosmic framework of Christ that is to such an extent inflated to embrace the whole of the natural cosmic world. She also did not follow as some Protestants in the footsteps of Hegel with a grand divine evolutionary rolling out from above of the absolute Spirit embracing the whole of human and cosmic history. White resolutely maintains and sustains the demarcation line between the divinity and humanity of the person of Christ. She extended Christ's view of truth and his way of his teaching to every phase of nature as employed by him in illustrating truth without the typical nineteenth fusion fashionable in many circles of her time:

> He taught that heaven and earth are linked together, and that a knowledge of divine truth prepares men better to perform the duties of everyday life. He spoke as one familiar with heaven, conscious of His relationship to God, yet recognizing His unity with every member of the human family (White [1898] 1948a, 19).

White, moreover, connects Christ's truth with nature in the most intrinsic sense of the word, but she never came anywhere close to any of the multiple Christ-centric cosmic approaches best represented by the Roman Catholic Teilhard de Chardin. He viewed the cosmic Christ as the superhuman real mover, directing an overall evolution process and the omega point at the end of time (Van Niekerk 2005, 155-159). White stays within the realm of Christ as the divine/human person who interprets his message:

> Christ interpreted the message, which He Himself had given to the lilies and the grass of the field. He desires us to read it in every lily and every spire of grass. His words are full of assurance, and tend to confirm trust in God . . . So wide was Christ's view of truth, so extended His teaching, that every phase of nature was employed in illustrating truth. The scenes upon which the eye daily rests were all connected with some spiritual truth, so that nature is clothed with the parables of the Master (White [1900] 1941, 19).

The *second trajectory* of White's faith reflexive pattern revolves around divinely set time periods from Genesis to Revelation, deeply engrained and embodied in what has been termed above as the divine historical textuality of the Bible. In all the dispensations, an aspect of the divine/human history as centrally embodied in Christ and embedded in the Old and New Testament through the Spirit emerges. In White's view during all dispensations, Christ's Spirit did not cease to communicate light to individual minds and to embody revelations in the sacred canon of the Bible from beginning to end:

> In harmony with the Word of God, His Spirit was to continue its work throughout the period of the Gospel dispensation. During the ages while the Scriptures of both the Old and the New Testament were being given, the Holy Spirit did not cease to communicate light to individual minds, apart from the revelations to be

> embodied in the Sacred Canon. The Bible itself relates how, through the Holy Spirit, men received warning, reproof, counsel, and instruction, in matters in no way relating to the giving of the Scriptures. And mention is made of prophets in different ages, of whose utterances nothing is recorded. In like manner, after the close of the canon of the Scripture, the Holy Spirit was still to continue its work, to enlighten, warn, and comfort the children of God (White [1888] 1990a, vii-viii).

The main faith reflection line throughout White's writings is to be viewed as a description of the biblical historical timeline and heavenly-earthly spatial demarcations within the biblical historical timeline expressed as different dispensations or covenantal periods. Within the ambience of each of the dispensations, White's divine template or paradigm of the linkage of heaven and earth in a double-sided sense as *through* Christ and *in* Christ is basically in operation in her faith reflexive description. White expressed the intrinsic linkage and unity of various dispensations and covenantal periods as expressive of one Gospel:

> There is no such contrast as is often claimed to exist between the Old and the New Testament, the law of God and the Gospel of Christ, the requirements of the Jewish, and those of the Christian dispensation. Every soul saved in the former dispensation was saved by Christ as verily as we are saved by Him today. Patriarchs and prophets were Christians. The Gospel promise was given to the first pair in Eden, when they had by transgression separated themselves from God. The Gospel was preached to Abraham. The Hebrews all drank of that spiritual Rock, which was Christ (White 1956b, 1061; *Signs of the Times*, September 14, 1882).

In one sense, Jesus has condescended and become a tabernacle of God and dwelled with humanity. He (Christ) has revealed God not only to us, but also to the heavenly angels (White [1898] 1948a, 19)—everything happens through Christ. In another sense, we as humans are in Christ as the tabernacle of God. The link we have with God is possible only through and in Christ in every dispensation of time. Through the brightness of God's light in Christ, God impressed upon Israel and on Moses, in the "Moses-dispensation," the exalted character of the law and the glory of the Gospel revealed through Christ:

> By this brightness, God designed to impress upon Israel the sacred, exalted character of His law, and the glory of the Gospel revealed through Christ. While Moses was in the mount, God presented to him, not only the tables of the law, but also the plan of salvation. He saw that the sacrifice of Christ was pre-figured by all the types and symbols of the Jewish age; and it was the heavenly light streaming from Calvary, no less than the glory of the law of God, that shed such a radiance upon the face of Moses. That divine illumination symbolized the glory of the dispensation of which Moses was the visible mediator, a representative of the one true Intercessor (White [1890] 1958a, 330).

White's stays with her reflection of faith within the outlines of the divine historical timeline of the Bible, by firstly reflexively linking the demarcation of heaven and earth's and divinity and humanity (and nature) *through* Christ and *in* Christ. Second, White's central operational template of faith reflexivity of *through* Christ and *in* Christ is also spread and diversified in different dispensations or covenantal periods.

Calvin's reflexive faith patterns are done within the dispensational realms of God's creation, which cover to a large extent the Old Testament, and God's redemption and reconciliation, which cover mainly the New Testament era. The well-known distinction of various covenants in the biblical historical timeline emerged mainly from seventeenth-century Calvinist orthodox John Cocceius (Koch) (1603-1669), a professor at the University of Leiden (Heussi 1971, 362). Cocceius' federal or covenant's theology was influenced by Melanchton, Bucer, and Calvin himself with his strong emphasis of the two reflexive covenantal realms of creation and redemption in which firstly one's reflexive patterns of faith are extracted, and secondly, in which reflection about God, human beings, and the natural world takes place.

The main representatives from the sixteenth century of a federal theology or a theology of various covenants—dispensations in the modern idiom—were Bullinger, Olevianus, and Ursinus. Cocceius elaborated and systematized in a dynamic sense different contractual or covenantal conclusions between God, human beings, and the natural world in the divine historical timeline of the whole of the Bible from Genesis to Revelation. Cocceius' arrangement of his systematic theology was not done in terms of different "loci," as was the common way of doing theology in Protestant orthodoxy, but in terms of the various biblical conclusions of covenants in different eras of the biblical historical timeline. The notion of the Kingdom of God as the determinative notion, stringing and connecting the various covenants together, was for Cocceius just as important as the notion of multiple covenants in different time periods of the biblical divine history. In spite of vehement reaction by strict Protestant orthodox protagonists, the support for and the influence of the notion of multiple contracts, covenants, and dispensations in the Bible between God, human beings, and the natural world never faded in many churches (Heussi 1971, 362).

Important with regard to White is that the seventeenth- to the eighteenth-century Puritan continuation of the sixteenth-century Calvinist branch in the New World influenced many movements in the nineteenth century. It is commonly acknowledged that the Puritan emphasis on the laws of God and the divine imperative of people's adherence and obedience to the laws of God influenced White on major points of her whole God-human-world approach.

A strong mixing of concepts from what has been called the Radical Reformation wing of the sixteenth-century Reformation with the mainline viewpoints of the sixteenth-century Reformation was already built into seventeenth- to the eighteenth-century Puritanism, in England and the New World. The pietist experiential views within the Puritan world came from both the sixteenth-century Reformation and Radical Reformation wing, as well as from eighteenth-century John Wesley through the Dutch Calvinist, Jacob Arminius, who is regarded in this work not as a non-Calvinist but as representing the "left-wing" of eighteenth-century Calvinism. In conjunction, the immense influence of John Wesley, who was heavily influenced by Arminius, is central in White's works, especially with regard to the centrality of Christ in all her works.

A merger and amalgamation of certain central notions of the Radical Reformation, as the left wing of the Reformation and the so-called mainline approaches of Luther and Calvin of the sixteenth-century Reformation as well as through formalistic, law-abiding Puritanism and pietistic pious Puritanism of the seventeenth and eighteenth century, produced a variety of influences on White's approach (Knight 2000, 30).

Firstly, White is not only influenced by the mainline sixteenth-century Reformation notion of *sola Scriptura*—Scripture alone—operationally in the works of Calvin and Luther, but also secondly, by the Radical Reformation rejected by Calvin and Luther. The radical Reformers of the sixteen century viewed biblical history as a virtual exemplar of what happens in people's everyday lives and to them the Kingdom of God was imminently coming and approaching from the future and was on the brink of being established amongst them in their times. Thomas Müntzer (1468-1525), one of the many radical Reformers, lived as pastor in Zwickau where a proletarian uprising due to social and economic circumstances was emerging. Müntzer, for instance, described infant baptism as a "beastly play of monkeys" (*viehische Affenspiel*). He reacted against Luther's doctrine of justification as a view of "gentle living spiritless flesh of Wittenberg" (*das sanftlebende geistlose Fleisch zu Wittenberg*) and biblical belief as "faith stolen from books" (*aus Bücher gestohlener Glauben*) (Bakhuizen van den Brink, and Dankbaar 1967, 98). Müntzer was killed in 1525 during the famous war of the small farmers suppressed by the governing princes, and in turn supported by Luther.

One obviously cannot bring White into the company of such harsh statements, but there are similarities. The whole approach of the Radical Reformers of viewing God as directly at work in their socio-historical circumstances combined with their belief that the Kingdom of God was on the brink of being established among them has a similar sound as the prophetic era around the 1840s in which the Second Coming of Christ was in real material terms expected to take place in the year 1844. White, as a young woman, was part of that experience. The fact that it did not happen was called the Great Disappointment. The difference with the mainline Reformation views of Calvin and Luther lies in the way history is experienced, not primarily through the proclamation of the Word of God, but also prophetically, materially and realistically as the present truth in the present experience of people, thereby indicating God's acts and works in the present as qualitatively similar, but also different from what is been depicted in and through the divine biblical historical timeline of the Bible.

Thirdly, White's view of dispensational eras in the biblical historical timeline displays the influence of the concept of multiple covenants and dispensations demarcated in the whole of biblical history. God's communicative love through and in Christ is the determinative notion in all White's works that strings and connects the various dispensations and covenants together, not primarily the notion of the Kingdom of God, as it was for Cocceius and for some of the later Puritans.

The influence of the Puritan mindset, values, and beliefs on White and Seventh-day Adventism has been extensively described by B. W. Ball's work, *The English Connection: The Puritan Roots of Seventh-day Adventist Belief* (1981), especially regarding unique notions like the ministry of Christ in heaven, Gospel obedience, and obedience to the laws of God—a future-directed apocalyptic view of prophecy that is anchored and comes true in God's divine historical events through history. As an appendix, the Seventh-day Sabbath can also be added to her Puritan roots. Ball compares similarities of several doctrinal notions between the Puritan sense-making world and that of White and Seventh-day Adventism, such as a) the sufficiency of Scripture; b) the incomparable Jesus; c) the righteousness of Christ; d) the new birth; e) believer's baptism; f) the heavenly ministry of Jesus; g) Gospel obedience; h) the Seventh-day Sabbath; i) the holistic nature of man; j) the return of Christ; k) apocalyptic prophecy; and l) the millennium, hell, and heaven.

Though Ball's portraying of similarities is on target and touches upon central features of White and Seventh-day Adventism, the main deficiency of Ball is the de-emphasizing of White and Seventh-day Adventism's concentration on the centrality of Christ within the full divine historical timeline portrayed as multiple-dispensational eras from Genesis to Revelation. White's faith reflexive patterning of the divine historical timeline is also influenced by the trajectory of the federal and covenantal dispensational eras of Cocceius and the later Puritanist protagonists of federal theology in the seventeenth to the eighteenth century.

The word, "dispensation," means an organized system, or method, by which affairs are conducted. The word is translated into English as "economy" and literally means "the law of the house." A political economy refers to the way the political affairs in the economic sense are being conducted during a set period. The political economic status of the nation addresses the financial affairs affecting a nation's money supply and commerce and the economic state of the citizens of the society. A dispensation, as used reflexively in the biblical sense of the word, is a period of time in which God was dealing with human beings in a particular way. For example, the first dispensation is called the Dispensation of Innocence and refers to Adam and Eve in the Garden of Eden before they sinned; it is viewed as a divine historical period. God dealt with Adam and Eve in the divine historical way in a particular way and told them to freely eat all the fruit in the garden, except the fruit of the tree of the knowledge of good and evil. Thus, in a dispensation or covenantal period of time, human beings have to live out their responsibility and be accountable to God, themselves, other human beings, and the natural world by obeying the laws, commands, and norms set by God.

These laws, commands, and norms are emerging through God's graceful and salvific acts set in a particular dispensation. The common way that people in our era make use of the laws, commands, and norms of a dispensation is either to mirror the divine and human acts, events, and doings of the particular dispensation in their lives or to interpret what these acts, events, and doings are actually and essentially portraying, and to apply the essential and interpreted prototypical core as divine examples in their lives of today.

Throughout the nineteenth century, certain forms of the notion of different divine dispensations built into the materiality of the divine historical timeline of the Bible emerged. The contractual and covenantal view of God's dealings with human beings of different contractual covenants in different periods for different purposes in the biblical historical timeline received special attention in the prophetic and Second Coming of Christ of people's experience in the nineteenth century. The whole idea of dispensations in the timeline of the Bible is a continuation in a different guise of the nominalist idea of the relationship in which God and human beings are facing each other in contracted or covenantal relationship.

In the sixteenth-century Reformation, with the seventeenth-century reformed orthodoxy in church experience and theological reflection in Europe, continued by the impact of the Puritan mindset in the New World, brought the notion about that God and human beings in their dealings in with each other concluded different successive contracts or covenants in different periods of biblical history. The main characteristic of these covenants in every era of biblical history is that they are one-sidedly set by divine action. A multiplicity of covenants emerged in the divinely set historical timeline of biblical revelation. The leap from the Puritan experience of an array of covenants set by God for his people is very short to the notion of dispensations in which God's children are tested in terms of a specific divine purpose intensively experienced in the nineteenth century, especially in the northeastern states of North America.

The best representative summary of a view of dispensations is the work of C. I. Scofield, who in his 1909 and 1917 editions of the Scofield Reference Bible, encapsulated various nineteenth-century views of divine revelational history, dispensations, and the divine historical linkages into seven dispensations. The New Schofield Reference Bible (1967, 3-4), closely following Scofield, states:

> A dispensation is a period of time during which man is tested in respect to his obedience to some specific revelation of the will of God. Three important concepts are implied in this definition, (1) a *deposit* of divine revelation concerning God's will, embodying what God requires of man as to his conduct; (2) man's *stewardship* of this divine revelation, in which he is responsible to obey it; and (3) a *time period*, often called an "age," during which this divine revelation is dominant in the testing of man's obedience to God.
>
> The dispensations are a progressive and connected revelation of God's dealings with man, given

sometimes to the whole race and at other times to a particular people, Israel. These different dispensations are not separate ways of salvation. During each of them, man is reconciled to God in only one, that is, by God's grace through the work of Christ that was accomplished on the cross and vindicated in His resurrection. Before the cross, man was saved in prospect of Christ's atoning sacrifice, through believing the revelation thus far given him. Since the cross, man has been saved by believing in the Lord Jesus Christ in whom revelation and redemption are consummated.

On man's part, the continuing requirement is obedience to the revelation of God. This obedience is a stewardship of faith. Although the divine revelation unfolds progressively, the deposit of truth in the earlier time periods is not discarded; rather, it is cumulative. Thus conscience (moral responsibility) is an abiding truth in human life (Rom. 2:15; 9:1; 2 Cor. 1:12; 4:2), although it does not continue as a dispensation. Similarly, the saved of this present dispensation are "not under law" as a specific test of obedience to divine revelation (Gal. 5:18; cp. Gal. 2:16; 3:11), yet the law remains an integral part of the Holy Scriptures, which, to the redeemed, are profitable for "instruction in righteousness" (2 Tim. 3:16-17; cp. Rom. 15:4).

The purpose of each dispensation, then, is to place many under a specific rule of conduct, but such stewardship is not a condition of salvation. In every past dispensation, unregenerate man has failed, and he has failed in this present dispensation and will in the future. But salvation has been and will continue to be available to him by God's grace through faith. Seven dispensations are distinguished in this edition of the Bible: Innocence (Gen. 1:28); Conscience or

> Moral Responsibility (Gen. 3:7); Human Government (Gen. 8:15); Promise (Gen. 12:1); Law (Ex. 19:1); Church (Acts 2:1); Kingdom (Rev. 20:4).

The backdrop of this view is that the first creative act of the heavens and the earth followed by the second creative act, animal life, and the third, human life, "refers to the dateless past" (Scofield 1967, 1). The notion of the dateless past informs the overbearing notion that the divine historical dating is revealed only through God's revelatory acts of the different dispensations. In each dispensation as a demarcated period of time, a different qualitative dimension of divine revelation is dominant in that a dimension of divine history is deposited in such a way in the particular time period that a subsequent dispensation builds in progression on the previous one and is dynamically divinely connected. The Bible portrays divine history in divinely set time periods in which human beings' obedience to God is tested.

The center of the whole salvation-historical dispensational exposition is Jesus Christ. Schofield is adamant that the different dispensations are not separate ways of salvation, but that God's grace through the work of Christ accomplished on the cross and vindicated in the resurrection is the revelatory deposit from which all dispensations find their center. The dialectic between divinely set revelatory history and the stewardship history of human beings in a certain time period comes to an end when the human race fails the test of obedience, while the period ends with dramatic divine intervention and judgment. On one hand, the apocalyptic mood among people at the end of a time period gives rise to an abundant number of prophets expressing what God expects from the people. On the other hand, the prophets could build only on what had divinely and by revelation been deposited in previous time periods. The central message to human beings in the acting out of their stewardship is the message of obedience to God.

A dispensation is the way God worked with human beings within a defined period of time. There is much confusion on the matter, and many have greatly misunderstood what has been understood under God's different dispensational economies. Most of the confusion comes from mixing or misapplying, according to dispensationalists, God's instructions in one dispensation with another. A prime example is confusing God's instructions and promises to Israel with those God made to be followers in the current age of the church. In the strong dispensational-inclined world, God made specific national promises to Israel. God, also according to such a scheme, promised—before the dynamics of history were set in motion—that the coming and emerging Messiah of Israel and the wider world would reign over the whole of the world, sitting on the throne of David in the prototypical and stereotypical Israelite sense of the word while endorsing and occupying the land God gave them in the name of the Messiah.

In terms of the common dispensational sense-making view, a dispensation is the way God works with human beings within a defined period of time; God made literal and unconditional promises to Israel. According to this approach to God's promises, these promises have never been fulfilled or nullified. The majority of Protestant churches from the sixteenth-century Reformation hold the view that God has done away with Israel, and they say that believers in the Church Age have inherited these promises in a manifold way. Pre-millennial views boil down to a rejection of what is called A-millennialism. The theological term of "A-millennialism" or "no" millennium amounts to precisely what it portrays: no millennium in the divine or human historical sense. Those entertaining a view of pre-millennialism recognize teaching that strict followers of the Bible literally inherit the land God promised to Israel, so they apply these Old Testament truths to the age of the church by giving them some "spiritualized" and allegorical meaning.

According to strong millennialists, the dispensation of the Tribulation and the Millennium are denied by a-millennialists. By corrupting Scripture in terms of millennialism, a-millennialism amounts to a robbing of believing supporters of the "blessed hope" of the soon and imminent return of Jesus Christ and deliverance from the wrath of God that will be poured out upon this earth. The confusion of God's promises in one dispensation with God's promises in another dispensation convolutes different dispensations of God's dealings with human beings. The different dispensations of God's dealings with human beings and the world should be clear and differentiated from each other; they should not be mixed and confused. The failure to understand that God works differently in different dispensations and qualitatively in different ways with people in a particular divine historical realm confuses them by not acknowledging the most important rule of reflexively reading Scripture—keeping the dispensations and ages of Israel and the church separate.

Most dispensationalists believe in seven dispensations of time or temporal periods. Some believe in the existence of eight dispensations of God's workings with human beings. The following is a list of these dispensations:

1. Dispensation of Innocence; Creation to the Fall of Adam
2. Dispensation of Conscience: From the Fall of Adam to the Flood
3. Dispensation of Human Government: From the Flood to Abraham
4. Dispensation of Promise: Abraham to the Giving of the Law at Mt. Sinai by Moses
5. Dispensation of the Law: Moses Till the Time of Christ
6. Dispensation of Age of the Churches: Pentecost Till the Rapture

7. Dispensation of Tribulation: Rapture to the Millennium
8. Dispensation of Millennium: One Thousand-Year Reign of Christ on Earth; Ends with the Great White Throne Judgment and the New Heavens and Earth Followed by Eternity

Seventh-day Adventists do not espouse to terminology or the typical doctrine of the rapture. Instead, Adventists teach about the literal Second Coming of Christ. Furthermore, there will be a thousand years in heaven of reigning with Christ.

Many dispensationalists mistakenly combine the Tribulation with the age of the church and show the last age as the Commonwealth or Kingdom Age or Millennium. A dispensation is understood as involving: 1) A test for a human being; 2) A human being's failure; 3) God's judgment; 4) A rule of life; and 5) A crucial event or crisis. In each dispensation, these five elements can be found.

The dispensations or covenantal eras are clear evidence of the grace of God, according to protagonists of the dispensational view. A human being in each instance of a dispensation failed the responsibility and accountability giving to him or her by God. With his or her failure comes God's judgment. With every judgment comes the offer of forgiveness and salvation. After a human being failed God in the Garden of Eden, God was the initiating agent who made the coats of skins and clothed them, thereby giving them a picture of the forgiveness of God and his grace (Genesis 3:21).

In extreme mirroring approaches, the divine historical embeddedness and embodiment of events described in the biblical text—for instance the dispensation of Moses—is viewed literally as an enclosed divine historical era where the laws, rules, and norms people must be accepted and followed. Not even a soft interpretation in the real sense is allowed because that would amount to either drawing into the Moses dispensation, such as the divine historical embeddedness and embodiment of events from another more important dispensation, or placing the total emphasis on one central dispensation, such as the Christ dispensation, as the main access area of reading backward and forward in the divine historical timeline the permeation of the central happening of God's communicative love in the life and the cross and resurrection of Christ.

White's approach to dispensations is dynamic and not formalistic and scholastic. Salvation in any age, from God's acts of creation to the fall of Adam and Eve and then to the period after the fall, are viewed by White as divine historical events embodied and embedded in the natural earthly realm with the accompanying human events and acts. In the same vein, she emphasizes various dispensations without going beyond the reflexive demarcation set by the perimeters and margins of divine-heavenly and earthly-human levels of the biblical historical timeline. In some instances, she connects dispensations, as with John the Baptist, who is the connecting link between the dispensation of the law and the prophets and the Christian dispensation:

> The prophet John was the connecting link between the two dispensations. As God's representative, he stood forth to show the relation of the law and the prophets to the Christian dispensation. He was the lesser light, which was to be followed by a greater. The mind of John was illuminated by the Holy Spirit, that he might shed light upon his people; but no other light ever has shone or ever will shine so clearly upon fallen man as that which emanated from the teaching and example of Jesus. Christ and His mission had been but dimly understood as typified in the shadowy sacrifices. Even John had not fully comprehended the future, immortal life through the Savior (White [1898] 1948a, 220).

White blends the events and activities of one dispensation with another dispensation, for instance, the way Christ permeates and affirms the dispensation of Moses with that of the Gospel:

> Christ, during His earthly ministry, emphasized the binding claims of the Sabbath; in all His teaching, He showed reverence for the institution He Himself had given. In His days, the Sabbath had become so perverted that its observance reflected the character of selfish and arbitrary men rather than the character of God. Christ set aside the false teaching by which those who claimed to know God had misrepresented Him. Although followed with merciless hostility by the rabbis, He did not even appear to conform to their requirements, but went straight forward, keeping the Sabbath according to the law of God (White [1917] 1943, 183).

White concentrates and put a more than usual emphasis on a certain dispensation or period in the biblical timeline than on others:

> The Last Period of Probation—The Gospel dispensation is the last period of probation that will ever be granted to men. Those who live under this dispensation of test and trial and yet are not led to repent and obey will perish with the disloyal. There is no second trial. The Gospel that is to be preached to all nations, kindreds, tongues, and peoples presents the truth in clear lines, showing that obedience is the condition of gaining eternal life. Christ imparts His righteousness to those who consent to let Him take away their sins. We are indebted to Christ for the grace, which makes us complete in Him (White 1957, 971).

In some of her works, White points to strong similarities of the qualitative sameness of certain principles in different dispensations—for instance those of piety, justice, and leadership:

> The same principles of piety and justice that were to guide the rulers among God's people in the time of Moses and of David, were also to be followed by those given the oversight of the newly organized church of God in the Gospel dispensation. In the work of setting things in order in all the churches, and ordaining suitable men to act as officers, the apostles held to the high standards of leadership outlined in the Old Testament Scriptures. They maintained that he who is called to stand in a position of leading responsibility in the church "must be blameless, as the steward of God; not self-willed, not soon angry, not given to wine, no striker, not given to filthy lucre; but a lover of hospitality, a lover of good men, sober, just, holy, temperate; holding fast the faithful word as he hath been taught, that he may be able by sound doctrine both to exhort and to convince the gainsayers" Titus 1:7-9 (White 1911, 95).

During the Gospel dispensation and after the closing of the canon, the Spirit continues its work:

> In harmony with the word of God, His Spirit was to continue its work throughout the period of the Gospel dispensation. During the ages while the Scriptures of both the Old and the New Testament were being given, the Holy Spirit did not cease to communicate light to individual minds, apart from the revelations to be embodied in the Sacred Canon. The Bible itself relates how, through the Holy Spirit, men received warning, reproof, counsel, and instruction, in matters

> in no way relating to the giving of the Scriptures. And mention is made of prophets in different ages, of whose utterances nothing is recorded. In like manner, after the close of the canon of the Scripture, the Holy Spirit was still to continue its work, to enlighten, warn, and comfort the children of God (White [1888] 1990a, viii).

A final example of White's use of the notion of a historical time period as a dispensation is the present time we live:

> The dispensation in which we are now living is to be, to those that ask the dispensation of the Holy Spirit. Ask for His blessing. It is time we were more intense in our devotion. To us is committed the arduous, but happy, glorious work of revealing Christ to those who are in darkness. We are called to proclaim the special truths for this time. For all this the outpouring of the Spirit is essential. We should pray for it. The Lord expects us to ask Him. We have not been wholehearted in this work (White [1923] 1962, 511).

Dispensations are not totally different ways or different divine historical time periods in which different salvific schemes or different methods of administering God's grace are divinely expressed.

White, in her nineteenth-century approach, goes way beyond Calvin by covering more fully the whole divine biblical horizon of creation—reconciliation in Jesus Christ and God's renewal acts in the era of the Spirit in the direction to the new heaven and new earth in God's ongoing act of fulfillment and consummation. Calvin operates mainly with two covenantal periods or dispensational realms. White is more dynamic by acknowledging more dispensational realms and periods within the divine historical timeline from God's creation to fulfillment. In her faith-reflexive pattern of faith, dispensational eras overlap and permeate each other without connecting too tightly and without distinguishing too strictly. She refers to Moses, the Gospel, and Spirit dispensations, among others. In each dispensation, God works with human beings, not only in a very particular and distinct way, but also in a very pertinent way. However, there is a radical permeation of every dispensational era by the central setting and embodiment of God's dynamic communicative love through and in Jesus Christ's life, cross, resurrection and heavenly ministration as God's primordial divine/human exemplar of how heaven and earth are contracted and combined.

The biblical historical trajectory of biblical history enfolds and embraces the whole series of events and happenings spanning the period from the creational beginnings of humanity and the world till the fulfilling ambience of the new heavens and the earth. This embracing historical rendition is elaborated and spelled out through the embrace and encapsulation of God's acts of creation, reconciliation, renewal, and fulfillment through all modes, fields, and dimensions of experience, as expressive of the Commonwealth of God in the Kingdom, Priesthood, and Prophetdom sense of the word.

We have seen White's central dialectic emerge in two trajectories. The first trajectory is the centrality of Christ in the dialectical duality of God and human beings in which God's communicative love is expressed through and in Christ as God's prototypical and exemplary contracted template of heaven and earth and of the essential core of every dispensation. White says in this regard:

> There is no such contrast as is often claimed to exist between the Old and the New Testament, the law of God and the Gospel of Christ, the requirements of the Jewish and those of the Christian dispensation. Every soul saved in the former dispensation was saved by Christ as verily as we are saved by Him today. Patriarchs and prophets were Christians. The

> Gospel promise was given to the first pair in Eden, when they had by transgression separated themselves from God. The Gospel was preached to Abraham. The Hebrews all drank of that spiritual Rock, which was Christ (White 1956b, 1061).

The second trajectory is the process of divine history expounded in the biblical and salvation historical timeline from Genesis to Revelation in time periods or dispensations. The strong trajectory of dispensational or covenantal eras established and demarcated in the biblical historical timeline in White's works emerged through being influenced by the mixing of biblical historical impulses from the official mainline Reformational and Radical Reformational worlds, as well as the mixing of impulses from the two sides of Puritanism—the formalistic law-abiding Puritan experiences and pietist Puritanism—in which the striving of certainty is achieved through increasing experience of piousness in a puritan version of holiness. Last but not least, one has to acknowledge the impulses of John Wesley, the advocator of the centrality of Jesus enfolded in a constant experiential realm of holiness, as well as Baptist New England Puritans and Anabaptist nineteenth-century movements and groups.

God's communicative love is expressed within the array of dispensations, but is not bound by them. White, in a message to teachers, emphasized the higher importance of God's love:

> Bible instruction is to be made forcible by the holy life of the teacher. God-fearing teachers will practice every principle they seek to imprint on the minds of the children. Such teachers do not see their heavenly Father except by the eye of faith; but they have learned of Him; they read His love in the most trying dispensations. They do not judge their Creator by dispensations; they are partakers of His divine nature. They can trust Him who withheld not His only-begotten Son, knowing that with Him He will

give all things for their spiritual and eternal good (White 1913, 183).

2.3 The Origins of the Trinity Notion and the Biblical Historical Timeline

2.3.1 Introduction

The speculative reflection on the operations of the three "persons" in the Godhead, differently portrayed and differently worked out, was a contributing factor to the split between the Eastern and the Western Church in 1054 CE. The problem with the notion of the Trinity is mainly twofold. First, the three persons of the Trinity in any theological reflection scheme is not strictly and directly linked to God's grand acts of creation, reconciliation, and renewal, not to speak of God's future-oriented act of fulfillment of everything. Secondly, the idea of God as one being that equals three beings, modes, processes, operations, or persons haunts any Trinitarian view, whether from the first millennium where it originated or the modern era.

Anyone accepting the sense-making logic of the first millennium notion of a "three as one" God or a "one as three" Gods lays the table for immense speculation that has very little to do with the grand acts of God in the biblical historical timeline. Many expositions and renditions of the notion of the Trinity were given the past two millennia, but they revolve around the idea of God as one being equals three beings, modes, processes, operations, or persons. The main speculation has its concentration point on the second leg as whether the three beings, modes, etc., were of the same ontological quality or had the same weight as God as one being. In many churches in the second millennium, an uneasy truce with this sense-making logic of the first millennium—that everything in their world, from God to human beings, had to be distinguished into three parts or sections—emerged.

The first millennium logic of a something that is equal to three things, but is also not equal to the three things with regard to God as a Trinitarian God found its main expression between 325 to 553 CE. At the church council of Nicea in 325CE, a small minority of church leaders decided that Jesus Christ is God. This council, under the forceful leadership of Emperor Constantine, who was out of political expediency not a Christian, at the time, lay the table for the centuries of Trinitarian speculation (Heussi 1971, 96). Now I must hasten to say that although this vote was not about whether Jesus was divine or not, (since he was deemed divine by his followers and the early church), it was to determine "*how*" divine he was in relation to God the Father (Ehrman 2004, 23). This truce that a minority of church leaders voted that Jesus is God at the Council of Nicaea, under the political monopoly of Emperor Constantine has recently been restated by Dan Brown in his controversial, *The Davinci Code.* Brown also stated that prior to the Nicene Council, the followers of Christ viewed him "as a mortal prophet…a great and powerful man, but a man nonetheless, a mortal" (Brown 2004, 315-316).

Lutzer pugnaciously responded with a formidable and plausible fight against Brown's insertion that, the divinity of Christ was voted and passed by a "relatively close vote." Said Lutzer, "That is fiction, since only five out of more than three hundred bishops (the number is actually believed to have been 318) protested the creed. In fact, in the end, only two refused to sign it. The outcome was not exactly a cliff-hanger" (Lutzer 2005, 8). Given that that may be so, one has to concede that, the out-come of that vote was not decisive enough to remove the Arianism belief. In Lutzer's own words, "Arianism continued to have its adherents, and subsequent emperors sided with whichever view suited them at the time" (Lutzer 2005, 8).

Brown is factually correct in stating that Constantine used the Nicaea Council through corrupt maneuvers for his political gain. History confirms that Constantine presided with dominance over the Council's proceedings (Walker 1985, 134). In his work, *A History of Christianity*: (2009, 214), MacCulloch says that it was Constantine, with the probability of the recommendation of his ecclesiastical adviser (the Spanish Hosius of Cordova), who suggested to the Council to declare the pronouncement of the statement *homoousios* "of one substance." Brown is partially correct in stating that Constantine used the Nicene gathering for his political agenda since all the historians that I have read concur that Constantine wanted a united Christianity so that he could have a united empire (Ehrman 2004, 23).

That said however, I must hasten to caution that there is a deceptive danger foiled in Brown's self-styled facts, in that, they are comingled with a sweet poison of fiction so subtly applied that unless one reads with the spectacles of discerning historical caution and a skill of deciphering between fact and fiction, one might land up lured, confused and deluded by the deceptive drug of science-fiction.

Brown is wrong in saying that prior to the Council of Nicaea, Jesus' followers had viewed him solely, as a mere prophet, a man with extra-ordinary talents but not as God (Brown 2004, 315). Unless Brown wrote this out of pure ignorance or fancy, this is sheer impudence and indeed blasphemy to God, to denigrate God's only begotten Son, as nothing more than a mere mortal. In my view, this is like someone walking on the edge of an abyss. As writers we should safe-guard the avenue of our impulsive statements, lest we risk ourselves of the inferno, simply for the sake of fortune and fame. The divinity of Christ is not a chimera. It is not a phantasmagoria, but a reality!

Here is fact: Jesus' followers viewed him as the Son of God prior to the Nicene Council of 325 CE. The historian, Bart D. Ehrman, in his book *Truth and Fiction In The Da Vinci Code* (2004, 15), says that the character Teabing in the book *The Da Vinci Code*, presents a confusing view to Sophie with regard to the discussion about Jesus' divine identity. Ehrman says that Teabing says Jesus' identity as God had not been accepted prior to the Council of Nicaea, yet on the other hand, he (Teabing) says that Constantine only accepted to the canon those gospels that were elevating the divinity of Christ.

The fact is, both the Gospels and the epistles recognize Christ as God. Paul in Philippians 2:5-7 says: Let this same attitude and purpose and [humble] mind be in you which was in Christ Jesus: . . . Who, although being essentially one with God and in the form of God [possessing the fullness of the attributes which make God God], . . . stripped Himself [of all privileges and rightful dignity], so as to assume the guise of a servant (slave), in that He became like men and was born a human being. *As quoted from the Amplified Bible (1987, 1384).*

Outside of the Bible writers, we have the Church Fathers that confessed Christ's divinity. Porlycarp of Smyrna who wrote to the Phillipians approximately AD 112-118, acknowledged Christ's divinity. Another is Justin Martyr, who was of Palestinian birth, around AD 100 and martyred in AD 165. After his conversion he defended the faith and wrote,". . . Son . . . of God the Father and master of all." To this list we can also add Irenaeus, who became the bishop of Lyons in AD177. Irenaeus, commenting on John 1:1 said, "all distinctions between the Father and the Son vanish, for the one God made all things through His word." And so did Tertullian (150-212), advocate that Christ was fully divine and human (Lutzer 2005, 9-10). Last but not least, Ignatius, one of the Christian Martyrs, wrote: There is one physician, both fleshly and spiritual, born and unborn, God come in the flesh, . . . from both Mary and God, . . . Jesus Christ our Lord (Ehrman 2004, 17).

What historically transpired here is, after Constantine had defeated Licinius, half of the empire fell under his dominion. It is there where he found another war. It was an old theological battle over "the Logos-theology" which had begun in Alexandria, purportedly, around the year 318. It was a battle over the "The Word or Son of God" and his nature in relation to God the Father. The debate which had persisted for approximately sixty years, challenged Christians in their understanding and expressions of how they viewed God. In Egypt, Alexandria, a persistent Presbyter – priest, named Arius presiding, over a "parish" in Baucalis, had become a renowned figure in the Alexandrian Church. He taught that the Logos though he was not like other creatures he was a creature whom God had called into existence "out of nonexistence." He also propounded, that there was a time when the Son did not exist. The Alexandrian Pope *(321?-328)* having heard the views of Arius presented between Arius and a certain teacher, decided to stop Arius. Although Arius was denounced as a heretic, his views did not go un-abated (Walker 1985:131-132).

The divided camp of Christianity found itself mainly under Athanasius and Arius. Those under the banner of Athanasius appealed to the gospel of Saint John 1:1, where Christ is declared to be emanating with God from the beginning and through whom all things were created. Arians on the other camp pointed to the Epistle to the Colossians which refers to "the first born of all creation." This implied to the Arians, that he must have been created. To solidify their view, the Arians quoted Tertullian who had attributed to the Son a time of beginning. Athanasius' and his group appealed to Origen who had declared the timeless generation of the Son (Bainton 1992, 96).

The controversy over the divinity and humanity of Christ was one of the core reasons for dissent and disunity among Christians at that time. This disunity among Christians sparked the most acrimonious fights. The contention was so deeply divisive that Constantine, with the purpose to unify Christianity and thus attempt a unified Empire, convened the Council of Nicaea 325 CE. He summoned all the bishops to the city Nicaea of Asia Minor (Walker 1985, 133-134). At that Council, the debate overwhelmingly swung against Arius who was declared a heretic. In spite of the fact that Arius had been granted a hearing to defend his thesis (that

Christ was more than human, but that he was not *fully God*),the delegation concluded that if Christ was not God, then he could not redeem humankind. They also reasoned that, in saying that Christ was an extraordinary creature, was contradictory to the scriptures that endorses him as creator of the heavens, the earth and all things seen and unseen whether it be dominions, powers and principalities as subscribed in Colossians 1:16. After affirming the divinity of Christ, the delegates debated over the nature of Christ's divinity in terms of whether he was in the Greek words, "similar" or "like" *homoiousion* [my word] to God the father or whether he was the "same" or of one substance *(homoousion)* as God the Father. The historian Eusebius posed his Christological view that Jesus was *similar* to the Father God. Interestingly, a theologian earlier mentioned, by the name of Athanasius, (although present but not invited to the proceedings of the meeting), upheld the belief that even the inclination of viewing Christ's nature to be *similar* to God the Father, was a misinterpretation of the biblical doctrine of the divinity of Christ. Marcellus, an Asia Minor bishop, who was representing Athanasius at the proceedings of the meeting, argued that Christ could only be God in the highest sense if he is the *same* as God. Constantine realizing that the tide of the debate moved in favor of the theologian Athanasius through his scholarly representative, the bishop of Asia Minor, suggested to the gathered bishops that they endorse the usage of the Greek word *homoousion, "one and the same."* This meant Jesus had the same nature as God The Father (Lutzer 2005, 5- 6).

The victory by the Athanasians was yet to be challenged. After the council had been declared in favor of the Athanasians and that Constantine had five dissidents banished with Arius included, and threatening with death those who would not handover their books, the emperor found that Arianism had dominated by its influence and teachings over the Christian majority of Asia Minor. Having as his main goal, unity, he agreed that the question be reopened. Hence, in 335 at a synod convened in Tyre, the subject of the divinity and humanity of Christ was re-examined. In short, the Arians won and Arius was restored while Athanasius was banished into exile (Bainton 1992, 97).

This theological warfare would later on continue. Constantine died in 337. The empire whose capital, he had moved to Constantinople prior to his death fell under the divide of his three sons. The provinces of the West were under Constantine II; The Middle-Africa, Italy, Greece and Rome were under Constans; and the East belonged to Constantius.

The religious beliefs of each district were adopted. The two brothers, Constantine II and Constans shared the same party and both held the Nicene dominance. The tide swept back when Constantine II died in a war of 340 and ten years later (350) his allied brother Constans was assassinated. This left Constantius ruling the entire empire. As a result of this, later on Saint Jerome (after observing this period) would say, "The world woke up to find itself Arian" (Bainton 1992, 97, 99).

However, in spite of that astonishing episode, history would witness a change when Constantius would die in 361. The empire was taken over by his notorious cousin Julian, whom history has renamed as Julian the Apostate. Julian who for a brief session led the Empire into a recession of paganism, ruled only for two years (361-363) (Bainton 1992, 99-100).

The Nicene come-back was given its "final victory" under the ruler-ship of the Spaniard Theodosius I. He called for the second ecumenical Council in Constantinople in 381. With minor amendments made, the Nicene Creed was reaffirmed.

Now I have dealt with the above in passing. It behooved me to deal with it as an indispensable necessity. While I do defend the idea that Christians prior to the Council of Nicaea viewed Christ as divine, I concede without controversy that the early Church has always been divided over their understanding over the divinity and humanity of Christ, especially so, in his relation to his "likeness" in substance and that of his "sameness" of substance to God the Father. This is also true with regard to how they differed over various other major doctrines (Riley 1997, 14).

What is of paramount importance for our study in this chapter, is to highlight the basic premise, already mentioned earlier, that the origins of the trinity notion, has been controversial in its formulation by the church councils from the offset.

At the council of 381CE in Constantinople, the addition of the Holy Spirit as God completed the notion of God as a Trinitarian God (Heussi 1971, 98). That the notion of the Trinity is controversial from the start is demonstrated at the council meetings of Ephesus in 431CE, Chalcedon in 451CE, and Constantinople in 553CE (Bakhuizen van den Brink 1965, 227).The 553CE council meeting "solved" the problem by aligning themselves with what they called the "Holy Fathers" and their four "Holy Councils."

These four council meetings received later special status as ecumenical meetings representative of the whole church of those days, which not one of the ecumenical councils were. About 600 CE, Pope Gregorian in Rome set the four ecumenical meetings on par with the four Gospels of the New Testament as cornerstones of Christian orthodoxy. Except at Ephesus, where bribery took place, the emperors mainly determined Christian doctrines.

At the beginning of the second millennium, the sense-making logic was changing. It is noteworthy that the earliest representative of the nominalist movement was Roscellinus of Compiegne in the eleventh century. He applied the early forms of nominalism to the doctrine of the Trinity and came to a denial of the unity of being of the three persons of the Trinity. His contemporaries accused him of tritheism (three Gods). Since the synod of Soisson in 1092 CE, where Roscellinus' views were condemned, nominalism was held as a heresy (Heussi 1971, 201). It was only in the fourteenth to the fifteenth century that nominalism re-emerged full force as the undercarriage of the sixteenth-century Reformation. Between the eleventh and fourteenth centuries, extreme realism was accepted by a neo-platonic minority and moderate realism by an Aristotelian majority (Heussi 1971, 201).

The nominalist procedure and program from 1100-1600 was a total changeover and subversion of the sense-making approach of the first millennium, with its perpetual classification system of threesomes and trichotomies of three levels, three substances, or three essences, into which every being, thing, and event was divided, even God. Their division was an approach that in broad terms simultaneously still let God face human beings and the natural world while letting God, human beings, and the natural world operate within the same realm or on the same level as the realm or the level of the world where we experience and experiment with God, ourselves, and things around us.

The scholastic and speculative approaches of the era from 1100 to 1600 operated fully with the first millennium notion of dividing and viewing God, human beings, and the natural world as operating on three cascading hierarchical levels of emergence and manifestation of *realness* and *logicalness*. The emergence and manifestation of realness and logicalness roll down from the top that is God, while the rising increase and ascending upsurge of realness and logicality start from bottom, that is, the natural world, to the top. The natural world and human beings are linked to God as the most real being and the most complete being full of logical possibilities.

The underlying sense-making intention of nominalism is best described as a late medieval revolution against the schemes of rising levels of increasing realness to more concrete and rising levels of increasing logicalness to more speculative and abstract substances and essences found in their completeness in God at the top of the scheme. These schemes no longer made sense in the new era because what the continuation of the old procedures in the new era did was to obfuscate and blur the experience of people regarding God, themselves, and the natural world. In the process of renouncing metaphysics by establishing physics in the study of the natural world, nominalism ventured to strip theology and the theological schemes, such as the notion of the Trinity, of all its distorting hierarchical speculative and high-above-the-world theological shackles. The result was that the Scriptures became the exploration area for faith reflection and extraction and acquirement of meaning for everyday life, and the notion of the Trinity as an operational hypothesis for daily life fell at the wayside. The result was that the prior decrees of God were emphasized, as they were seen to be operationally embodied and embedded in the world at the expense of speculation about God as the most real being and the most thoughtful being from whom we have to derive our thoughts, beliefs, and meanings for everyday life.

The new image of God emerging from the approach, which in broad terms simultaneously still let God face human beings and the natural world while letting God, human beings, and the natural world operate within the same realm or on the same level of the world, is that of the covenantal God, who through his self-commitment in his *pactum* or *foedus* becomes the contractual partner in creation and salvation. If a human being stands before God as a contractual partner whom God has accepted and pledged to reward, a human being is no longer a second cause moved by God, but the first cause—the prime mover of all things in the world and in the church. In other words, God is no longer directly causing and working packages of qualitative realness and pockets of meaningful thoughts in the world of human beings and the church; a human being received his or her own role before God. In this new sense-making approach, a human being has become the appointed representative and partner of God, responsible for his or her own life in the broader society, the church, and the world, on the basis and within the limits of the treaty, *pactum*, or covenant stipulated by God (Oberman 1986, 29).

The carrier notion of the nominalist program is the notion of contingency and contingent, meaning the reality and the world we live in is full of incidental occurrences and individual things. In the nominalist program, this should be understood in two directions, embracing both the vertical relation God-human-world and the horizontal relation past-world-human-future. Reality and the world full of incidental occurrences and individual things happening and set within the ordered framework of God's power should not be seen as unreliable and unrelated accidental occurrences and things. In the vertical dimension of God-human-world in nominalism, Godly factors are Godly factors; human factors are human factors; and natural worldly factors are natural worldly factors. In the horizontal dimension of past-world-human-future, an alternate form of contingent and contingency opens up of a complexity of human and natural worldly factors added to divine factors in the course of events viewed in the past or toward the future.

Very seldom in history is, in a linear historical sense, God the Father linked to the act of creation; God as Son linked to reconciliation; and God the Spirit linked to God's act of renewal, beginning with Pentecost in the biblical timeline. When the linkages of Father, Son, and Holy Spirit with creation, reconciliation and renewal had been concluded, and different directions were attempted, either the notion of the Trinity, broke into three Gods or viewed as one God with three operational ways—that is, a creational, reconciliatory, and renewal operational way—or the notion of a threesome in any way, totally disappeared in favor of the notion that there is one God with thousands of dimensions, sides, and ways.

2.3.2 Calvin and the Trinitarian Problem

It flows from this state of affairs that Calvin emphasized the realms of creation and reconciliatory salvation as his main biblical reflexive realms in which God, human beings, and the natural world are reflected upon (Van Niekerk 2009b, 42-43). Calvin's main sense-making line of operation is the biblical salvation historical timeline following the grand acts of God. However, though, Calvin emphasized creation and reconciliation more than God's acts of renewal and fulfillment. The notion of the Trinity in the broader scheme of the grand acts of God in Calvin's work is a bit extraneous, even though he (Calvin) asserts that the Trinitarian view of God plays a strong role in his *Institutes of the Christian Religion* of 1559 (1960a, 13).

If one operates like Calvin, with the notion of the Trinity as one God with three persons, Father, Son, and Holy Spirit ([1559] 1960a, 13), one cannot link the three persons successively to God's divine historical acts of creation, reconciliation, renewal and fulfillment. The divine historical timeline (creation, reconciliation, renewal and fulfillment) is the ground structure of Calvin's main theological reflexive realms of creation and reconciliation in which God, human beings, and the natural created world are reflected on, in the sense of the one not without the other. Calvin, as many before and after him, was employing the notion of the Trinity of one God in three persons as a guarantee for the unity of God and God's actions, thus, for example, reading Christ or the Spirit into most obscure texts in the Old Testament.

It is also clear that the notion of the Trinity is an auxiliary construction for Calvin's main procedure of working in the biblical historical timeline. Calvin, when he writes about the Trinity, takes on the garb of the church tradition and states lamely that those expressions such as "Trinity" and "person," applied to God, aid the interpretation of Scripture and are therefore admissible. He further adds that the Church in history has regarded expressions like "Trinity" and "person" as necessary to unmask false teachers. Remarkably, Calvin uses his exposition of the Trinity to demonstrate how biblically grounded the notion of the Trinity is. Biblically, it is expressive of God's "infinite and spiritual essence." Calvin, however, did not venture into the question of how the respective persons of the Trinity are to be linked to the grand acts of God (creation, reconciliation, renewal and fulfillment) [1559] 1960a, 13).

Calvin's continuation with the traditional doctrine of the Trinity in his work is also at odds with his notion of what others called his *extra-calvinisticum* tendency. The term "extra" in the phrase demonstrates the extra in Calvin's work—extras not to be found in the writings, sayings, and doings of his fellow Reformers in the sixteenth century. *Extra-calvinisticum* meant, for Calvin (and Zwingli), that Christ, after his ascension, still had his resurrected humanity and full humanness with him (Weber [1962], 1981-1983, 153; Van Niekerk 2009b, 36). Thus, Christ is not present through his own actions, but through the Holy Spirit, who applies the cross and the resurrection of Jesus as the present-making and saving tools of God in this world, in churches, and in people's lives. According to Van Niekerk (2009b, 37), Servetus, who was sent to die at the stake by Calvin, had views of the Trinity that were surprisingly closer to the thrust of Calvin's *extra-Calvinisticum* than Calvin's own views on the Trinity. Calvin's Trinitarian formula, if he was to be consistent with his idea of the *extra-Calvinisticum*, should have been something like the following: God the Father; God the divine and human Son; and God the Holy Spirit.

The contradiction in Calvin's work resulted from an alignment with ancient church doctrines, such as that of the Trinity, while Calvin himself strongly emphasized the Bible as his main exploration area for reflection on God, human beings, and the natural world. While Calvin's emphasis on the biblical historical timeline, embracing the grand acts of God's creation and reconciliation, stems from the sense-making ambience of the new realism of nominalism and Renaissance humanism of his era, the notion of the Trinity is a full-fledged first millennium doctrine that emerged from the ecclesial and political struggles of that era.

Calvin, while working in the anti-scholastic ambience of Renaissance humanism and nominalism, was not sufficiently aware that by accepting the Trinitarian doctrine of the scholastic church tradition with its speculative coordinates, God was thereby positioned outside God's own grand acts. A human theological construction came to life as the Trinitarian God in the church tradition. The main problem with the notion of the Trinity is that the constructed realm of theologians portrayed in church doctrines as the three-in-one divine beings in action in and through the Trinitarian God is set above God's grand acts of creation, reconciliation, renewal, and fulfillment. When the Trinitarian God is, in some way or other, connected to the biblical timeline, theologians use the term "economical Trinity." For the Trinity above and outside the biblical timeline, the term "ontological Trinity" is used. The terms ontological and economic Trinity are another way of applying the bifocal procedure of reflecting simultaneously on the "inside" and "outside" of God.

2.3.3 White and the Trinitarian Problem

Early Seventh-day Adventists rejected the notion of the Trinity. The notion of the Trinity never played any determinative role in White's reflection on the biblical historical timeline, as it has functioned as an operational tool for theological speculation in many other theologies and doctrinal reflection of many of the mainline churches. She, however, alludes to the "three living persons of the heavenly trio" (White [1946] 1970, 615). Her reflection in *Evangelism* ([1946] 1970, 613-617) suggests that she believed that the Scriptures taught the existence of three co-eternal divine persons. White also states in *The Desire of Ages* that:

> Sin could be resisted and overcome only through the mighty agency of the Third Person of the Godhead, who would come with no modified energy, but in the fullness of divine power (White [1898] 1948a, 671).

In the current world, there is a deliberate attempt to view the last phase of White's writings as determinative regarding the notion of the Trinity. This is arrived through an interpretative unlocking of the developmental line in the Seventh-day Adventist world about the notion of the Trinity from the early anti-Trinitarian views to the shift and turn White made in 1898 with her work *The Desire of Ages*. The real problem arises when the notion of the Trinity is superimposed on White's work as her main working hypothesis, denying her immense contribution and unlocking of the biblical historical timeline in the nineteenth- and twentieth-century world and replacing it with an unhistorical Trinitarian dogma of three divine persons.

Moon asserts regarding the developmental line of White that:

> Her writings about the Godhead show a clear progression, not primarily from anti- to pro-Trinitarianism, but from relative ambiguity to greater specificity. Some of her early statements are capable of various interpretations, but her later statements, 1898-1906, are explicit to the point of being dogmatic (Moon 2003b, 278).

In the current Seventh-day Adventist world, three periods of development regarding the notion of the Trinity from the early beginnings are acknowledged. For clarity's sake, we follow the exposition of Moon in his two essays on the Adventist Trinity Debate (2003a and 2003b) distinguishing the following three periods:

2.3.3.1 The First Period of Anti-Trinitarianism: 1846-1888

Moon summarizes the reasons for the early rejection of the notion of the Trinity as the following:

1. Early Adventists did not see biblical evidence for three persons in one Godhead.
2. They thought the Trinity made the Father and the Son identical.

3. They believed the misconception that the doctrine of the Trinity teaches the existence of three Gods.
   J. N. Loughborough stated, for example, in 1861: "If Father, Son, and Holy Ghost are each God, it would be three Gods" (quoted in Moon 2003a).
4. They believed the doctrine of the Trinity would diminish the value of the atonement.
   J. H. Waggoner (1884): Since the "everliving, self-existent God" cannot die, then if Christ had self-existence as God, he couldn't have died on the cross (quoted in Moon 2003a).
5. The fact that Christ is called "son of God" and "the beginning of the creation of God" (Revelation 3:14) was thought to prove that he must be of more recent origin than God the Father.
6. The variety of expressions used to refer to the Holy Spirit indicates that *it* could not properly be considered a person.

Moon's conclusion about these reasons boils down to the following statement:

> These arguments made sense within an overall anti-Trinitarian paradigm, but when that paradigm was called into question, these points were recognized as being capable of fitting either interpretation. None of these is a valid objection to the basic Trinitarian concept of one God in three Persons (Moon 2003a, 118).

A closer reading of each of these reasons points to the sense-making nineteenth-century Adventist ambience of experience from which these arguments emerged. They were not born out of an anti-Trinitarian or an anti-mainline church mindset. Rather, they arose out of an extremely strong emphasis on the biblical historical timeline as the area of all reflection (theology) about God, human beings, and the natural world.

Moon accepts too easily "the basic Trinitarian concept of one God in three Persons," the *Deus est Trinitas* of the ancient Church doctrine (Barth [1932] 1975, 350) as a broad working hypothesis. The first millennium logic of the Trinity as a closed system notion is under extreme pressure from wholesome sense-making views of our era that discovered the time-space reality of the biblical historical way of reflection about God, human beings, and the natural world. In this regard, early Seventh-day Adventists and White of the early period were precursors in directing the way to the unlocking of a biblical historical reflexive way of theological discourse.

The first argument that early Adventists did not see biblical evidence for three persons in one Godhead is underwritten by no other than Karl Barth, who used the notion of the Trinity as one of the grounding structures of his own theological dogmatics:

> Already in the early Church, the doctrine of the Trinity was attacked on the ground that it is not biblical, that in the form in which it was formulated by the Church's theology it cannot be read anywhere in the Bible. This is especially true of the crucial terms "essence" and "person," which theology used. But it is also true of the word "Trinity" itself (Barth [1932] 1975, 308).

Barth continues by saying that:

> The Bible can no more contain the dogma of the Trinity explicitly than it can contain other dogmas explicitly . . . We cannot prove the truth of the dogma that is not as such in the Bible merely from the fact that it is a dogma, but rather from the fact that we can and must regard it as a good interpretation of the Bible (Barth [1932] 1975, 310).

The second argument of early Adventists who "thought the Trinity made the Father and the Son identical" is born out of the experience of people who adhered to the divine biblical historical timeline as the operational area in which and through which God (the Father) worked. The early Adventist world, which was strongly directed to the fulfillment at the end of times, found with sense-making necessity the notion of "three equal partners that is actually one" in the Trinity a nonsense-making exercise. The problematic notion of the Trinity, which probably made sense to many in the first millennium, is carried forward by the mainline churches to the end of the second millennium as a central doctrine. In our era, at the start of the third millennium, large cracks appear in the edifice of the Trinitarian doctrine in a widespread sense in many mainline churches. More than a hundred years ago in the nineteenth century, Adventists already demonstrated the problematic nature of the doctrine of the Trinity. The way they did it was firstly to bypass the age-old argument of Trinitarian theologians with the greatest ease that one has to accept the mystery of the "three-in-one" God, not with logical arguments but in faith. Secondly, their strong emphasis on the divine historical timeline of the Bible made the doctrine of the Trinity obsolete.

The third argument of early Adventists, who "believed the misconception that the doctrine of the Trinity teaches the existence of three Gods," was not actually a misconception. Church history is full of struggles, especially around the notion of the Trinity as expressive of three Gods. Apart from the practical experience of many in various churches that the Trinity amounts to the existence of three Gods, the early Adventists operated in terms of Jesus Christ as the central scope of the biblical historical timeline. Barth, in the twentieth century, operated in a similar manner, by reducing and concentrating the biblical historical timeline from Genesis to Revelation into the midst of history in Jesus Christ as God's central and only revelation.

The fourth argument of early Adventists, who "believed the doctrine of the Trinity would diminish the value of the atonement," is born out of their experience of atonement in Jesus Christ as the central scope of the biblical historical timeline as set out between the first and the imminent Second Coming of Christ.

The fifth argument of early Adventists, that "Christ is called 'son of God' and 'the beginning of the creation of God' (Revelation 3:14), was thought to prove that he must be of more recent origin than God the Father." Though problematical as an argument in the general sense of the word, it is an honest acknowledgement of the quality of the divine historical timeline presented in the Bible—that the Father could more be linked to creation and Christ as the Son of God with atonement and reconciliation.

The sixth argument of early Adventists, that "the variety of expressions used to refer to the Holy Spirit indicates that *it* could not properly be considered a person," has as an underlying argument. The metaphors and images with which the workings and actions of the Spirit as God's Spirit are described in the biblical historical timeline demonstrate the characteristics of instrumentality and organic action of God.

Moon is correct in viewing these arguments as anti-Trinitarian, but what he is not realizing is that any version of the first millennium notion of a Trinitarian God cannot be easily fitted into the nineteenth-century emphasis of a divine historical timeline covering the Bible from start to finish. Except for various populist reasons against the notion of a Trinity, such as that some Evangelical Christians are questioning traditional Trinitarianism and that some Adventists believe church leaders and theologians sold out the "original" Adventist belief on the doctrine of God for the sake of public relations and ecumenical goodwill, there is another reason found in Calvin, which is remarkably similar to the notion of the Trinity as "one God in three divine persons." That notion fits in very problematically with Adventist and White's views. If Christ is a divine and human being, and if the divinity and humanity are closely aligned but not mixed, then Jesus Christ as divine and human Son of God is totally different from the sole divine Son of God of 99 percent of Trinitarian schemes in history. The Trinity is not actually operational in Calvin's reflection, especially in his *Institutes* of 1559, in spite of innumerable attempts to defend him in this regard. A sensible conclusion of Calvin's Trinitarian views, either by himself or by others, should actually have read, "God as Father, God and Human as Son of God and God as Spirit." This would clearly make the classical Trinitarian dogma of *Deus est Trinitas* unworkable.

2.3.3.2 The Second Period of Dissatisfaction with Anti-Trinitarianism: 1888-1898

According to Moon, the 1888 emphasis on righteousness by faith and the consequent exaltation of the cross of Christ called into question whether a subordinate, derived divinity of Christ could adequately account for the saving power of Christ. This period can be regarded as the period in which the ambiguity between Adventism's emphasis on the biblical historical timeline of the Bible and the notion of the Trinity was at its peak.

In 1890, E. J. Waggoner expressed this ambiguity with his insistence to "set forth Christ's rightful position of equality with the Father, in order that His power to redeem may be better appreciated." He also states that Christ has "life in Himself; He possesses immortality in His own right" (Waggoner 1890, 19-22). The more the divinity of Christ was emphasized and the lesser his humanity, the more Trinitarian Waggoner's views became and the less he was reflecting in terms of the historical timeline of God's salvation work. It is clear from Moon's following statement that to be Trinitarian in one's reflection means it is necessary to have three divine persons on a par in what a Trinity should be:

> Waggoner was not yet fully Trinitarian [by 1890 when he wrote his book *Christ and His Righteousness*], but he saw clearly that a more exalted conception of Christ's work of redemption demanded a higher conception of his being as Deity (Moon 2003a, 113-129).

The omission of a "higher conception of his being as a man," meaning more human, is not part of Moon's reflection on this period. In the same period, White, in a letter to Waggoner and Jones in 1887, spoke a different language than Moon (and Waggoner) did:

> It was poverty that as He passed to and fro among the subjects He came to save, scarcely a solitary voice called Him blessed, scarcely a solitary hand was stretched out in friendship, and scarcely a solitary roof proffered Him shelter. Then look beneath the disguise, and whom do we see?—Divinity, the Eternal Son of God, just as mighty, just as infinitely gifted with all the resources of power, and He was found in fashion as a man (White [1888] 1987, 28).

The importance of this quotation, especially the part"—Divinity, the Eternal Son of God . . ." could be viewed as anti-Trinitarian because of the close alignment of divinity and humanity in the eternal Son of God in the disguise and fashion as a man.

2.3.3.3 The Third Period of the Paradigm Shift: 1898-1915

White, on the other hand, in the nineteenth century, lived in a world where the sense-making experience of the notion of the Trinity had already been experienced as something far away from biblical history and the biblical historical salvific timeline. It is not a question of followers of White as to whether she denied or fully embraced the notion of the Trinity. The notion of the Trinity, to a large extent, is not White's main operational hypothesis. Her emphasis is on the divine historical timeline of the Bible from Genesis to Revelation, which made the doctrine of the Trinity, as the majority of mainline churches professed it, redundant in her writings. White and other Seventh-day Adventist members who underemphasized the notion of a Trinitarian God—and some who even rejected the Trinity—were closer to the biblical historical timeline than the majority of mainline churches who fully acknowledge the notion of a Trinity as a central doctrine, but whose members in their daily lives experience very little of what is reflected about in the abstract heights of theological Trinitarian reflection.

White's main approach of reflection is concretely embedded in biblical reflection on the grand acts of God's creation, reconciliation, renewal, and fulfillment. In terms of her main approach, the notion of the Trinity as an operational hypothesis plays a secondary role, even more secondary than in Calvin's approach. The debate around White in the later part of her life as a fully-fledged Trinitarian protagonist in line with the Trinitarian dogma of the *Deus est Trinitas* has to be conducted in terms of the main thrust of her sense-making God-human-world view. That is, she was always reflecting within the ambience of the divine historical timeline expressed in the portrayal of God's grand acts of creation, reconciliation, renewal, and fulfillment.

The discussion around her full-fledged Trinitarian views follows this route of argumentation: Though White did not at first recognize God's Trinitarian nature from the beginning of her ministry, she portrayed God as a personal, literal, and tangible being, in contrast to "spiritualizers" and deists who viewed God as a distant, impersonal, mystical, and ultimately unreal being. Contrary to this argument, one has to state that it is not a question of White not recognizing the widespread acceptance of the Trinitarian doctrine in many churches, but that her focus was to follow the divine historical timeline of God's grand acts as markers for the realm in which she reflected on God, human beings, and the natural world. The latter way of doing is precisely what she did not find in the notion of the *Deus est Trinitas* hovering, in a speculative sense, above God's grand acts as portrayed for her in the biblical historical timeline.

The advocators of White as a Trinitarian supporter proceed by arguing that when White changed her views, as she did in the 1890s and 1900s, God was described as real individual persons of Father, Son, and Holy Spirit. Thus, she emphasized their *threeness* as willing, thinking, social, and relational persons, and explained their *oneness* in terms of nature, character, purpose, and love, but not in terms of being one person.

Moon, in his extensive work on the growth pattern of the Trinitarian notion of God in White's writings, states:

> There is a clear progression from the simple to the complex, suggesting that Ellen White's understanding did grow and change as she received additional light (Moon 2003b?, 284).

Granted that there are various growth patterns and various developing themes and issues in White's life, one has also to be aware that any categorization of terms, words, notions, and metaphors she used in her writings, sayings, and doings in different eras of her life has to acknowledge and recognize the underlying theme of the divine biblical historical timeline continuously reflexively demonstrated and illustrated through the grand acts of God's creation, reconciliation, renewal and fulfillment. White's sense-making God-human-nature approach in a specific work, and in her works as a whole, should theologically be investigated in terms of her emphasis on the reflexive realm of the divine historical timeline of the Bible.

Caution has to be exercised. One has to be extremely aware regarding the notion of a Trinitarian God still doing the rounds in the modern world. In other words, danger lurks in those areas of speculative theological reflection about the essence of God and should not be opened in the current Seventh-day Adventist world simply for the purpose of ecumenical recognition by mainline church theologies. On the other hand, concrete theological reflection based on the grand acts of God of creation, reconciliation, renewal, and fulfillment as illustration and demonstration of the biblical historical timeline should be enhanced and taken more seriously than has thus far been the case. We have seen how Calvin was not consistent with his "add-on" of the *Deus est Trinitas* to the biblical historical reflexive realms of creation and reconciliation (redemption). How much more could it be said of White, who in a stricter sense, adhered to the full biblical historical timeline than Calvin? The whole speculative tradition of the notion of "God as one in a threesome" brings the strict connection of Christ's divinity and humanity in the grand act of God's reconciliation into a problem area of gigantic proportions. Thus, if we accept the notion fully—that the one God comprises three divine persons (*Deus est Trinitas*) as Father, Son, and Holy Spirit—what then are we to do with the humanity of the Son, which in a post-incarnation sense is never to be loosened again from his divinity in both Calvin's and White's views? Although, in Calvin's view, the humanity of Christ is ultimately lost in infinity, as we saw earlier, we must ensure that there is no confusion here. Of all the strange views of Calvin and White, the strangest of them all, to various other church traditions, is probably this view of the continuation of the close combination of divinity and humanity of Jesus Christ far into the farthest end of eternity.

There is some debate about whether the current Adventist view of the Trinity is following the classic Trinitarian formula of the *Deus est Trinitas*. In this regard, Moon, in a presentation at the Adventist Theological Society's 2006 Trinity Symposium, asserts of White's Trinitarian views:

> She taught that the Father, Son, and Holy Spirit are three distinct individuals, which is not true of the medieval doctrine of the Trinity (http://atsjats.org/site/1/podcast/06_Trinity_Moon_Quest_Biblical_Trinity.mp3).

The view presented by Moon at this point is closing in on the notion of Tritheism and is remarkably close to the views of the nominalist Roscellinus of Compiegne in the eleventh century, which has been referred to previously (Heussi 1971, 201). Roscellinus's early nominalism, to a certain extent, annunciated the second millennium's sweeping logic of twosomes while bringing officially the first millennium's sweeping logic of threesomes into a binary scheme of God facing human beings within the same realm. Because early nominalism of the eleventh century, and later nominalism of the fourteenth to the sixteenth centuries, operated not with the typical threesome sense-making view cascading on three levels but brought God, human beings, and the natural world within the same realm, their sense-making logic, when applied to the Trinity, nearly always led to three persons, as with Roscellinus; three processes, such as with Servetus in Calvin's era; and three individuals, into which shoes Moon shoves White into.

As had been said earlier in this work, White stays within the divine historical outlines of the divine biblical historical timeline. She operates everywhere reflexively in her works with the linkage of the demarcation of heaven and earth and divinity and humanity (and nature) facing each other in close proximity *through* Christ and *in* Christ. This reflexive operational mode of White specifically and particularly is applicable to her nineteenth-century "nominalist" view of the divine threesome she refers to in different parts of her works. It is noteworthy that the notion of "heaven-earth intrinsically linked in Christ" is everywhere at work in the majority of her reflexive sections, even in the few reflexive considerations she construed about the notion of the Trinity. The centrality of the "heaven-earth connection in Christ," as the operational reflexive mode of operation, is not only spread over and diversified in different dispensations or covenantal periods, but also is central in her remarks on the notion of a threesome partnership of God.

Remarkably one can surmise that Moon and others if they are not fully aware of White's anti-speculative stance, deliberatively underemphasize White's stance of concrete and practical faith, reflexive description of the actions, sayings and doings of God within the ambience of the divine historical timeline of the Judeo-Christian Bible.

There is a continuous and determinative drive amongst some of my fellow Seventh-day Adventists such as Woodrow Whidden, Jerry Moon, and John Reeve, to find the idea of the Trinity in the deepest sense of the word biblically proven. To them, the biblical evidence for a Trinitarian God is espoused by the fact that both the Old Testament and New Testament contain indications that the One God is not merely solitary, and that the New Testament explicitly refers to Father, Son, and Holy Spirit, albeit in different contexts (see, e.g., Matt 28:19; 2 Cor 13:14) (Moon 2003a, 125).

In well described turns and phrases, Moon gave a rendition of the long process amongst Seventh-day Adventists, which he regarded as starting out with an anti-Trinitarianist stance—grounded in Scripture to a turned around stance, advocating the basic concept of *one God in three persons*—also indeed founded in Scripture and of which he coincidentally is a strong supporter:

> The long process of change from early Adventists' initial rejection of creedal trinitarianism to their eventual acceptance of a doctrine of the Trinity could rightly be called a search for a biblical Trinity. They were not so much prejudiced against traditional formulas as they were determined to hew their doctrine as closely as possible to the line of Scripture. In order to base their beliefs on Scripture alone, and to disenfranchise tradition from exercising any theological authority, they found it methodologically essential to reject every doctrine not clearly grounded in Scripture alone. Since the traditional doctrine of the Trinity clearly contained unscriptural elements, they rejected it. Eventually, however, they became convinced that the basic concept of *one God in three persons* was indeed found in Scripture (Moon 2003a, 123-24).

One does not have to be extraordinarily gifted to see that anti-Trinitarianism as well as Trinitarianism in the classical sense of the word has an immense difficult task to find itself grounded within the pages of the Judeo-Christian Bible. It is worthwhile to repeat what we have quoted earlier of Karl Barth, the great twentieth century neo-orthodox Reformed theologian, regarding the doctrine of the Trinity. Barth acknowledged that the doctrine of the Trinity was not biblical, especially in the form it was formulated by the theology of the Church in general, and that it cannot be read anywhere in the Bible. Barth adds that it is especially true of the crucial terms "essence" and "person," which theology used. But it is also true of the word "Trinity" itself (Barth [1932] 1975, 308).

Barth continues to assert on a later page that the Bible can no more contain the dogma of the Trinity explicitly than it can contain other dogmas explicitly. The proof of a dogma is not as such in the Bible because it is a dogma but from the fact that we can and must regard it as a good interpretation of the Bible (Barth [1932] 1975, 310).

The following four quotations from White's *Special Testimonies*, *The Upward Look*, and *Sons and Daughters of God*, regarding a Trinitarian notion are exemplary concerning her anti-speculative stance. They also reveal that she was neither anti-Trinitarian nor was she a typical traditional Trinitarian with its static speculative views, but rather that she was a dynamic Trinitarian, open-ended:

> The Lord Jesus Christ, the only begotten Son of the Father, is truly God in infinity, but not in personality (White 1982b, 367).
>
> But not from the stars or the ocean or the cataract can we learn of the personality of God as it is revealed in Christ (White 1955, 21).
>
> The Father is all the fullness of the Godhead bodily, and is invisible to mortal sight. The Son is all the fullness of the Godhead manifested. The Word of God declares Him to be "the express image of His

> person . . . God so loved the world, that He gave His only begotten Son, that whosoever believeth in Him should not perish, but have everlasting life." Here is shown the personality of the Father (White [1946] 1970, 614).
>
> The Comforter that Christ promised to send after He ascended to heaven, is the Spirit in all the fullness of the Godhead, making manifest the power of divine grace to all who receive and believe in Christ as a personal Savior. There are three living persons of the heavenly trio; in the name of these three great powers—the Father, the Son, and the Holy Spirit—those who receive Christ by living faith are baptized, and these powers will co-operate with the obedient subjects of heaven in their efforts to live the new life in Christ (White 1906, 63).

It is interesting to observe her use of the two words "is" and "bodily" regarding the Father as the fullness of the Godhead; the two words "is" and "manifested" regarding the Son as fullness of the Godhead; and the two words "is" and "making manifest" regarding the Spirit, as in all the fullness of the Godhead. The centrality lies in Christ regarding "divine grace," "believe in Christ as a personal Savior," "those who receive Christ by living faith are baptized"—in the name of the heavenly trio and powers—"cooperating with the obedient subjects of heaven in their efforts to live the new life in Christ." A classical speculative view of a Trinity is not emphasized here, but heaven and earth are bound together in Christ. One has to read the elaborate quotation above in conjunction with the way in which in Christ, divine history and ordinary history, God and human beings, and heaven and earth are inextricable connected:

> In Christ, the family of earth and the family of heaven are bound together. Christ glorified is our brother. Heaven is enshrined in humanity, and humanity is

> enfolded in the bosom of Infinite Love (White [1898] 1948a, 25-26).

Any strict advocator of the notion of the Trinity as White's final and determinative view emerging in the later part of her life should take the following into account: First, that White, not being a speculative theologian, avidly applied metaphors and images in her reflection, which she mainly extricated from the Bible as the biblical historical exploration area of reflection. Secondly, we must take cognizance of the context from which and in which she portrays and describes a certain view. Thirdly, many of White's references and reflective utterances on the notion of the Trinity had to do with her strong biblical reflective experience of "God speaks" (*Deus dixit*) as a God of love.

God, as a speaking God of love, is overall in action in White's writings, sayings, and doings. God's love is not a reflective scheme in her works, but the phrase "God is love" as God in action appears repetitively first and foremost in her major books. A good example of the loving God in action is her use of the phrase "God is love" as the first three words in the first volume of the Conflict of the Ages Series (*Patriarchs and Prophets*) and the last three words of the final volume of the series (*The Great Controversy*). The many references to the notion of the Trinity in her works are encapsulated under the loving God's speaking and not the other way around.

Finally, it is remarkable if one meanders in an investigative sense through the contexts in which references to the notion of a Trinity appear. In nearly all of these instances, she was reacting to speculative views of others regarding God's nature or where a dualist view of God was presented or where a mixing of God and human beings were propagated or where God and the natural world were fused in a pantheistic sense, as in her opposition to the views of Kellogg.

Great reflexive schemes and grand doctrines were not her intention; she was portraying and describing God speaking in the real and actual sense as the loving God. The absolute scarcity of quotations, in the overall scheme of her immense productivity of either expressed statements against or in favor of the Trinity, set within a speculative dogmatic framework, is evidence of her concrete reflective and anti-speculative focus.

The immense contribution White and Seventh-day Adventists made to the Christian world, and thus the Kingdom of God, lies first in the nineteenth century changeover, from a reductionist emphasis advocated by many churches, on God's grand acts of creation and reconciliation to a stronger emphasis on all God's grand acts of creation, reconciliation, renewal, and fulfillment viewed and reflexively rolled forth in terms of the biblical historical timeline.

2.4 Epilogue

We should constantly be aware that in Calvin's and White's approaches, the reflection is done within the margins of the biblical historical timeline in which the grand acts of God's creation, reconciliation, renewal, and fulfillment are portrayed. Though Calvin and White have considerable differences, each in his and her own way reflexively speaks about God continuously in direct relationship with human beings and the natural cosmic world. Their emphasis on the divine historicalness of the biblical timeline is the main reason why so little speculative and fanciful scholastic notions are found in their work. They concentrate their reflection on God, not in isolation from human beings and the natural world, which are, so to speak, Calvin's and White's other reflexive partners of the triad and which are intrinsically involved in the reflection exercise that is carried out.

The concentration on the reflection of God's grand acts in the biblical timeline brought a dissonance between Calvin's view of how each of God's grand acts of creation, reconciliation, renewal, and fulfillment is to be connected in turn with his view of the Trinity. Already in Calvin's time, it was clear in the aftermath of the Renaissance that the Trinity, which flowed from a first millennium sense-making logic, is with great difficulty to be linked with God's grand acts of the biblical timeline. With the glory of hindsight, we see that Calvin was not aware that linking the notion of the Trinity with God's grand acts created a dissonance in his sense-making approach.

The fact that White, who lived in an era where the Trinity was a topic of theological tussle, conspicuously, omits, in all her voluminous writings, the word 'Trinity' and succinctly employs etymologically the word "Trio" instead, is to me not co-incidental , but intentional. White's somewhat deliberate by-passing of the Trinity notion with all of its speculative, controversial, theological pitfalls, is doing what I call, pre-meditated, purposive avoidance. She did not want to be strapped and clamped down by the paralysis of analysis of the Trinity. Her reflexive sense making logic of God helped her to reconnoiter her position, which prevented her, from being dragged down by the gravity and depravity of the Trinity in its traditional formality. Without controversy, she used the basic Trinitarian formula as tools and a vehicle to communicate God's love to humanity, without conforming to its limitations it poses in as far as it relates to the biblical historical timeline. She operated with a notion of divine historicity of the biblical timeline in an era where the second millennium sense-making logic was already in full swing and experienced from the beginning of her ministry in the nineteenth century problems with the notion of the Trinity. The debate whether White, in her later views on the three persons of the Trinity, is aligning with the tradition of the Church or whether she is presenting a new way of reflection on the notion of three persons of the Trinity is not yet settled. What is certain is that White did not fully support anti-Trinitarian views analogous as she did not support full-fledged classical Trinitarian views. The closest we can get to White's view about the Trinity is to call her an open-ended Trinitarian, thereby fully acknowledging her emphasis on the grand acts of God in the length and breadth of the divine historical timeline.

CHAPTER 3

The Centrality of God's Grand Act of Reconciliation in Jesus Christ

3.1 Introduction

In this chapter, the views of Calvin and White on the centrality of Jesus Christ as God's act of reconciliation, redemption, and salvation are discussed. What has been termed the second problem-setting to be discussed in this work revolves fully around Jesus Christ's life, death, and resurrection as central within the array of God's grand acts from beginning to end. In another way, this problem-setting could be described as the vertical and horizontal divine/human axis of divine history played out in Jesus Christ from creation to fulfillment.

In order to understand how Calvin and White perceived Jesus' life, his death, and his resurrection as centrally placed within the array of God's grand acts of creation and renewal through the Holy Spirit of Pentecost and God's consummation and fulfillment of all things culminating in the new heaven and the new earth, the entire scenario of God's grand acts is viewed here through a Christ-centric focus. Thus, some of the more important facts of the great plan of salvation, reconciliation, and redemption in the controversy between good and evil are described.

One of the attempts of this book is to ascertain what the true identity of Jesus Christ signifies. Does the biblical account we are referring to consist of real, factual, and historically described real events and happenings? Is it secular historical, mythical science fiction? Or is it to be discarded through historical scientific factuality as consisting of trumped up narratives? As far as it relates to Calvin and White, the biblical account is made up of real, literal, historical, and factually reported documents.

In what follows, three access areas are opened up regarding the principles underlying Calvin's and White's descriptions of the astounding mystery of the identity of the natures of Christ.

3.1.1 The First Access Area: Interactional Substantialism

The first access area is that of the equity of the dual natures in the person of Jesus. Calvin and White, regarding the equity of Christ's true, dual nature, are discussed as representatives of the *interactional substantialist* approach. Three other approaches, *transformational trans-substantialism, con-substantialism*, and *human-mono-substantialism* or *monothelitic substantialism*, are cursively dealt with as limiting notions in describing how Christ was seen by others in history.

As we already stated, Calvin's Christology, like White's, keeps a distinction of the two natures that are mysteriously combined into one person. Calvin purported and propounded on the Christological notion that the humility of Christ is demonstrated by him, being born in a stable, which allows us to see glimpses of his glory from his baptism up to his crucifixion, resurrection, and ascension to the right hand of the Father. At this stage, we have to assert that the main pre-suppositions of Calvin and White, regarding the two natures of Jesus has strong paradoxical elements built into it.

Many modern groups since the Enlightenment of the eighteenth century have interpolated the dual divine and human personhood of Christ with underlying assumptions and allegations defining him as an ordinary man with extraordinary talents. The main assumption is that he is only and exclusively human with a degree of God's presence in him. This is representative of the *human-mono-substantialist* viewpoint. However, other Christian groups with a more traditional stance have continued to affirm both of Jesus' dual natures—his divinity and humanity. Therefore, in this part of the work, we will mainly deal with rhetorical and Christological comparisons between Calvin and White. The modern liberal humanistic view, which regards Jesus as consisting of a *human-mono-substantialist* nature, will be treated in passing.

3.1.2 The Second Access Area: Perpetual Mediatorship

The second access area concerns the role and place of Jesus Christ in the divine history from Genesis to Revelation. The continuing and perpetual mediatorship of Christ, stretched over the biblical timeline, is of importance here. In the opening up of this assumption as an operative principle in the work of Calvin and White, the divine biblical historical period from the pre-existence of Christ to the post-existence of Christ at the right hand of the Father is also of importance.

The perception of the dual natures of Christ, housed in one person, gives rise in terms of Calvin's and White's writings to the second main assumption of a dynamic, ongoing, and perpetual interactional substantiation of the two natures. The operative principle here is that Jesus acted out his divinity sometimes and at other times his humanness in his life, death, and resurrection. At times, divinity was made manifest through his total humanness, and at other times, divinity withdrew, allowing for his utter humanity to come to the fore. What this means is that Jesus' identity demonstrated interactional exactions of *quiescent divinity* and *active divinity.*

3.1.3 The Third Access Area

The third access area, which functions as an operative principle in the writings of Calvin and White, is that of a multidimensional approach to the titles, offices, and dimensions of Jesus Christ.

3.2 Jesus Christ: Dual Nature

3.2.1 Calvin on Christ's Dual Nature

Earlier in this work, we discussed how a whole array of dualities fitting into each other in Calvin's writings are derived from and are expressive of his main duality of the knowledge of God, the creator, and the knowledge of God, the redeemer. Calvin's main dualities, that of a "vertical," *mirroring*, reflexive, double layeredness between heaven and earth, divinity and humanity, and a "horizontal" reflexive, *processual* duality between Genesis and Revelation, beginning and end, creation and fulfillment, are expressive of the biblical historical timeline (Van Niekerk 2009b, 42).

With regard to the duality of the two natures of Christ in Calvin's approach, Christ is set on one hand as the combined, dual, divinely particularized and concentrated divine/human mediating prototype between God and human beings, between heaven and earth, as the mediator that intercedes for us before God. And, on the other hand, within the biblical historical timeline, Christ is centrally placed as the divine/human mediating archetype between God's act of creation at the beginning of time, and God's act of fulfillment at the end of time, and is therefore simultaneously fully involved in God's acts of creation, reconciliation, renewal, and fulfillment at the end of time. The main emphasis in Calvin's approach is the two covenantal periods or dispensational realms of creation and reconciliation expressed within the Old and New Testament: reconciliation (redemption) acquired in Calvin's approach, the pivotal and prototypical position between creation in the past and consummation in the future through a linkage with the Holy Spirit. Calvin effectuates a link through his emphasis on Christ as the perpetual mediator interceding between God and human beings in a continuous sense until the future fulfillment at the end.

Regarding the duality of Christ's natures, Calvin notes in his *Institutes* of 1559:

> When it is said that the Word was made flesh, we must not understand it as if he were either changed into flesh, or confusedly intermingled with flesh, but that he made choice of the Virgin's womb as a temple in which he might dwell (Calvin [1989] 2001b, 415).

We notice in the aforementioned words of Calvin a striking parallel of what exists in various passages in the Bible. We read in Exodus 25:8, for example, the existence of an idea of an infinite God who is depicted as one who dwelled in an earthly temple. It is this idea of the pre-existent, omnipresent Son of God whose presence, though was and still is universal, remained and continues to be distinct and manifest at a certain fixed locality. Calvin understood the "mechanics" of Christ's dual participation in the equality of the "persons" of the Trinity while he (Christ) was simultaneously also a participant in his human body and earthly existence. To Calvin, the justification of the unification of Christ's divinity and humanity can be conceptualized in the notion of being miraculously co-descendent of God's Son:

> From heaven, yet without abandoning heaven; was pleased to be conceived miraculously in the Virgin's womb, to live on earth and hang upon the cross, and yet always filled the world as from the beginning (Calvin [1989] 2001b, 414).

Calvin's and later Ellen White's approach of the strong duality of the natures of the one person, Jesus Christ, was different from the central Roman Catholic notion of *transubstantiation*, in which the divine Son of God is transformed into a sacramental and sacred divine human being, Jesus Christ. Both Calvin and White differ from the main Lutheran notion of *consubstantiation*, in which the human Jesus is constantly permeated by his divinity and appears thereby as an actualized and permeated-diffused human God. One has to point to the fact that the view and experience of Christ among Catholics, Lutherans, Calvinists, and Seventh-day Adventists are mostly encountered not in the handbooks of their main theological representatives, but in the everyday experiences of their followers within the faith codes and modes, rituals, and forms operating and functioning in their churches. It seems as if Christians worldwide view Christ as a real mystery within the approaches of their churches.

In Calvin's view, the mystery of Christ revolves around "how" the two natures of Christ's person existed in a co-existent and somewhat stogy way without being mingled or fused. Although Calvin operated strongly with the mystery of the combined, but not mixed, unity of the two natures of Christ, he attempted to explain the mystery through the example of the two main components he regarded of which a human being consists. He mentioned that as a human being is a composite of a body and a soul, which as substances cannot be confused and fused into one substance, a human person stays a composite duality in being a single person. In a similar sense, the divine and human natures of Christ are expressive of the one person of Christ (Kerr 1989, 73).

Calvin refers also to the "what" of the status of Christ's divinity. In essence, Calvin answered this question above when he asserted that while Jesus was on earth, Christ remained a divine partner of the triune God. According to Calvin, Jesus did not cease to be an active partner in dealing with the affairs of the universe while he was on earth as a human being, nor did he cease to be God at his death. In my view, Calvin's concept of Christ's identity as a duality of contra-natures in the one person of Christ seems to be from the same stream that Ignatius drank from. Ignatius said that Christ dined with his disciples in flesh while he was simultaneously "united" with his Father in Spirit (www.earlychristianwritings.com/text/Ignatius=smyrnaeans=longer.html).

The question of what happened to Christ's person, in becoming flesh, at the incarnation is of importance at this stage. Did Christ, in other words, take upon himself a human body that was tainted by sin? Here Calvin is cautious and introduces an exception, wrought by divine intervention. According to his theory, the Holy Spirit *sanctified* Christ at conception, which immunized him from being contaminated. Calvin further clarifies that the ubiquitous being as the Word of God was not contained in the bosom, since he continued to fully inhabit the universe. This is how Calvin states his position:

> For we make Christ free of all stain not just because he was begotten of his mother without copulation with man, but because he was sanctified by the Spirit that the generation might be pure and undefiled as would have been true before Adam's fall. And this remains for us an established fact: whenever Scripture calls our attention to the purity of Christ, it is to be understood of his true human nature, for it would have been superfluous to say that God is pure (Calvin [1559] 1960b, 13).

If we asked Calvin, what happened to Christ's divinity while he (Jesus) was weeping over Jerusalem, as reported by Luke 19:41-44, Calvin would propose that Christ's divinity was *resting*. In a similar vein, one could ask Calvin what was Jesus' divine nature doing while his human nature was suffering excruciatingly at the cross? Calvin's answer is emphatically, simplistically, concisely coined in one word—*quiescent* (Edmondson 2004, 198).

The stance of Calvin, in which Christ's resurrected humanity is still with him in "heaven" at the right hand side of the Father, has been called the *extra-Calvinisticum*. The notion "extra," in the composite term, points to what is extra to Calvin's views and what is not part of the other Reformers of the sixteenth-century Reformation, though it was a position also held by Zwingli, the Swiss Reformer.

In a famous portion of his 1559 *Institutes*, Calvin describes the whole notion of the *extra-Calvinisticum* by describing how the Word of God became flesh:

> They thrust upon us as something absurd the fact that if the Word of God became flesh, then he was confined within the narrow prison of an earthly body. This is mere impudence! For even if the Word in his immeasurable essence united with the nature of man into one person, we do not imagine that he was confined therein. Here is something marvelous: the Son of God descended from heaven in such a way that, without leaving heaven, he willed to be born in the virgin's womb, to go about the earth, and to hang upon the cross; yet he continuously filled the world even as he had done from the beginning! (Calvin [1559] 1960b, 13).

The notion of the *extra-Calvinisticum* caused vehement reaction in Calvin's time. Some of the objections came from Lutheran theological scholars who rejected the *extra-Calvinisticum*. The heart of the *extra-Calvinisticum* is that Christ still has his resurrected humanity with him where he is presently situated at the right-hand side of the Father (Van Niekerk 1984, 34, 58-69).

The Lutherans objected, both against the idea that Christ in his present state ascended to the right hand side of the Father and still has his resurrected humanity as part of him and against the notion that Christ is only present through the Holy Spirit in people's lives and in the physical natural world. What they were concerned about in Calvin's doctrine of incarnation was that it made it possible for Christ eternal to be God's Word not to be separated from the incarnated Christ having Christ's humanity intrinsically and inseparably always as part of him. They feared and saw it as a real threat that people could no longer speak of a *logos asarkos*, in which Christ exists and is positioned externally from his human body.

Although the discussion of Calvin regarding the unity of the divine and human natures of Christ sounds totally in line with the Chalcedonian type of argumentation, there are real differences that are carried by his making use of the notion of *alloiosis* in his approach. Calvin starts with his discussion by stating that the statement that "the Word was made flesh" in John 1:14, cannot be understood:

> That the Word was turned into flesh, or confusedly mingled with flesh. Rather, it means that, because he chose for himself the virgin's womb as a temple in which to dwell, he who was the Son of God became the Son of man—not by confusion of substance, but by unity of person. For we affirm his divinity so joined and united with his humanity that each retains its distinctive nature unimpaired, and yet these two natures constitute one Christ (Calvin [1559] 1960d, 17).

In a typical Calvinian manner, Calvin proceeds to undergird the mystery of the two contracted but not fused and mixed natures of Christ with his basic assumptions as to how the mystery is to be worked out in terms of soul and body as two substances of a human being:

> If anything like this very great mystery can be found in human affairs, the most apposite parallel seems to be that of man whom we see to consist of two substances. Yet neither is so mingled with the other as to not retain its own distinctive nature. For the soul is not the body, and the body is not the soul. Therefore, some things are said exclusively of the soul that can in no way apply to the body; and of the body, again, that in a way fit the soul; of the whole man, that cannot refer—except inappropriately—to either soul or body separately. Finally, the characteristics of the mind (*animus*) are [sometimes] transferred to the

> body, and those of the body to the soul. Yet, he who consists of these parts is one man, not many. Such expressions signify both that there is one person in man composed of two elements joined together, and that there are two diverse underlying natures that make up this person (Calvin [1559] 1960d, 17).

Calvin finalizes his description of the mystery of two substances joined but not fused and mixed by applying this whole train of reflection to the two natures of Christ:

> Thus, also the Scriptures speak of Christ: they sometimes attribute to him what must be referred solely to his humanity, sometimes what belongs uniquely to his divinity; and sometimes what embraces both natures but fits neither alone. And they so earnestly express this union of the two natures that is in Christ as sometimes to interchange them. This figure of speech is called by the ancient writers "the communicating of properties" (Calvin [1559] 1960d, 17).

What Calvin refers to is the figure of speech of the *alloiosis*, carrying the communication of properties. Lutherans were concerned that such a union of Christ's two natures presented by Calvin, and especially by Zwingli, through the notion of *alloiosis*, would spell that the human nature could not have divine attributes (Edmonson 2004, 198-214). There was a great debate in the sixteenth-century Reformation around the notion of the *communicatio idiomatum* as the interchange, exchange, and fusion of properties and characteristics between the divine and human natures of Christ. In the theological debate that ensued later, the impression was created that the notion of the *communicatio idiomatum* has more or less the same meaning among the Reformers, because they all adhered to the line of Chalcedonian orthodoxy. It is of the utmost importance to position a Reformer's use of the notion of the *communicatio idiomatum* within a Reformer's sense-making God-human-nature approach. Even Calvin and Zwingli, supposedly closer to each other than to other Reformers, had slight differences that were of importance in the broader scheme of their sense-making approaches. In general, the notion of *alloiosis* expresses more the idea of similarity than of sameness of the divine and human natures of Christ.

3.2.2 White on Christ's Dual Nature

White's view of Christ's dual nature is worked out in terms of the outlines of her sense-making, God-human-nature approach. Earlier, we spelled out the double-layered divine-heavenly and human-earthly reality portrayed by White as that:

> In Christ, the family of earth and the family of heaven are bound together. Christ glorified is our brother. Heaven is enshrined in humanity, and humanity is enfolded in the bosom of Infinite Love (White [1898] 1948a, 25-26).

Through God's communicative infinite love in Christ, God and human beings are closely connected, concentrated, and contracted, and in Christ emerges the divine/human template of how God is connectively working within his grand acts of creation, reconciliation, renewal, and fulfillment. Christ in and through the divinely set time periods, or dispensations, from Genesis to Revelation is the central embodiment and manifestation of God's love.

White's view of Christ bears some similarity to that of Calvin, but with considerable differences. Although White is believed by many—particularly members of the Seventh-day Adventist Movement—not to be a systematic theologian, she has developed a view of the biblical historical timeline in which the centrality of Christ could be seen as the main result of the divine expression of God's communicative love. Unlike Calvin's approach to Christ, which is totally enveloped in the strong maintenance of his scheme of a divine/human duality, White is moving a bit freer in her approach from heaven to earth and from earth to heaven, thus from divinity to humanity and from humanity to divinity, but consistently within the same coherent reflexive frame of divine historical making.

In saying the above about White, I do not want to convey the idea that Calvin's view of Christ is totally one-sided. There are times when Calvin's Christology could be viewed from a perspective from above, from below, and from a salvific perspective. A similar exchange of perspectives, though in a slightly different way, holds true for White, who delves deep into Christ's pre-existence and post-existence and gives reasons as to why Christ assumed a lowly position. White's writings have a great deal of the holy and lofty position, in contrast to the lowly position that Christ, according to White, voluntarily assumed.

Before we take a look at the more detailed aspects of White's concept regarding Christ's divinity and humanity, let's give a brief summary of some important points with regard to Christ's divine and human natures, that is, his identity. White makes it clear that Christ held a position second to his Father. The nature of Christ remains a mystery for her even though she claims to having seen him in visions on several occasions:

> I have often seen the lovely Jesus, that He is a *person*. I asked Him if His father was a person and had a form like Himself. Said Jesus, "I am the express *image* of My Father's *person*" (White, AL 1985, 80).

In order to establish his identity, it is indispensable that we know where he is from, and possibly, know his age. When we attempt to know *what* part of, or *how* much of, eternity Christ assumes, White furnishes the following answer:

> From all eternity, Christ was united with the Father . . . The Word existed as a divine being, even

> as the eternal Son of God, in union and oneness with His Father (White 1958b, 248).

White also writes:

> Christ was God essentially, and in the highest sense. He was with God from all eternity, God over all, blessed forevermore. The Lord Jesus Christ, the divine Son of God, existed from eternity, a distinct person, yet one with the Father. He was the surpassing glory of heaven. He was the commander of the heavenly intelligences, and the adoring homage of the angels was received by Him as His right (*Review and Herald*, April 5, 1906).

Christ's identity to White is dynamic because in his identity, he is not only a mediation between his divinity and humanity, but he is also the exemplar of God's communicative infinite love to human beings and the natural cosmic world.

But to restate our question in our first access area: Did White perceive the identity of Christ as a divinized humanity? The answer is that White, like Calvin, does not perceive the identity of the human nature of Christ to have been divinized. She posed her rhetorical question in this manner:

> Was the human nature of the Son of Mary changed into the divine nature of the Son of God? No, the two natures were mysteriously blended in one person—the man Christ Jesus. In Him dwelt all the fullness of the God-head bodily (White [1953] 1985a, 444).

When we come to explaining "how" this was possible—that Jesus could be both God and man in the one person Jesus Christ—White admitted that it is a mystery that is unfathomable: "We cannot explain how divinity was clothed with humanity." However, that did not stop her from attempting to explain this great mystery. In an effort to describing how this took place, she wrote:

> Laying aside His royal robe and kingly crown, Christ clothed His divinity with humanity, that human beings might be raised from their degradation and placed on vantage-ground. Christ could not have come to this earth with the glory that He had in the heavenly courts. Sinful human beings could not have borne the sight. He veiled His divinity with the garb of humanity, but He did not part with His divinity (White [1953] 1985, 648-649).

As already mentioned earlier, according to White, Christ is not two separate persons, but one person with two natures mysteriously combined. She breaks down this tremendous mysterious complex identity of Christ as follows:

- His divinity is clothed by the garb of his humanity.
- He could not come and accomplish his redemptive work in his form of divinity.
- He divested his form of God and assumed a human form.

The question of how these complexities could be built into the identity of the person of Christ stays the great mystery that not only White, but Calvin, too, is confronted with. White contrived a decisive impasse to ensure that we are not deluded into entertaining the notion that there is a confused co-mingling of divinity and humanity in the person of Christ. We are not to think that his divinity was in any way degraded to our humanity; instead, we are to believe that divinity retained its position.

In a remarkable sense, Christ did not call upon his divine nature to relieve him of his unbearable burden. We may see an indirect form of divine intervention through what one might call a substitute for our substitute in the person of Simon of Cyrene, who by coercion had to carry the cross of Christ. One of the points I wish to make here is that, according to White, there was an indirect divine intervention present that helped Christ endure and helped alleviate the burden of the cross: "He could not carry the cross." However, it is important to note that although Christ received help through divine providence, he did not zoom into his divine nature. In his suffering, divinity was quiescent, and God sent Simon to help Jesus carry the cross (White [1898] 1948a, 742).

On one hand, having been ministering on earth, he did not give up his divinity; for he was still God. While on earth, he could immediately differentiate right from wrong. When he was tempted, his divinity flashed through. It was this mysterious combination of his divinity and his humanity that made it possible for him to withstand the fiercest temptations. On the other hand, in calming the storm at the Sea of Galilee, he did not do it as God but as a human being. He exercised his faith in God, leaving an example for us to follow. Christ assumed human nature and the liabilities thereof. He was tempted at all points and bore the sins of the world, and will always retain his humanity through ceaseless ages (White [1961] 1989, 49; 1964, 292; *Review and Herald*, October 11, 1881).

To the question, "What happened to Christ's divinity, when he died at Golgotha?" White says that only his humanity perished. His divinity never sank and died since that could never be a possibility.

A. As man, he could suffer death but not as God. It was therefore his humanity that died, since it is impossible for a deity to die.
B. As human, he could identify with suffering and sinful humanity.
C. As God, he could lift humanity to God.

To the question, "What happened to the natures of Christ at the incarnation?" White responds:

> He was to take his position at the head of humanity by taking the nature but not the sinfulness of man (White [1953] 1985, 448; White: *Signs of the Times*, May 29, 1901).

This was a position also held by Henry Melville, who was one of White's preferred authors. It was Melville who wrote that while Jesus had assumed humanity, he took the innocent infirmities, excluding the evil and sinful propensities. Added Melville:

> Here Deity interposed. The Holy Ghost overshadowed the Virgin and, allowing weakness to be derived from her, forbade wickedness; and so caused that there should be generated a sorrowing and a suffering but nevertheless an undefiled and spotless humanity, a humanity with tears, but not with strains; accessible to anguish, but not prone to offend; allied most closely with the produced misery, but infinitely removed from producing cause (Melville (pg 47), as quoted in General Conference of Seventh-day Adventists 1988, 57).

3.3 Christ's Identity as Mediator and Substitution

3.3.1 Calvin's View of Christ As Perpetual Kingly Priest and Mediator

Bearing in mind that since sin had separated us from the presence of God, according to Calvin, it necessitated only one who "belongs to God" to serve as our *intermediary*. No one from the sons and daughters of Adam could reach out to God. It required the Son of God to become "Emmanuel, God with us." In his commentary on Romans 8:34, Calvin writes:

> *Who is he that shall condemn?* As no one can succeed in his accusation when the judge absolves, so there remains no condemnation, when the laws have been satisfied and the penalty already paid. Christ is the One who once suffered the punishment due to us, and thereby professed that he took our place in order to deliver us. Anyone, therefore, who desires to condemn us after this must kill Christ Himself again. But Christ has not only died, He has also come forth as conqueror of death and triumphed over its power by His resurrection. Paul adds still more—Christ he states, now sits at the right hand of the Father. By this he means that He obtains dominion over heaven and earth, and full power and rule over all things, as he states in Eph. 1:20. Lastly, he teaches us that Christ is seated in this way in order to be a perpetual advocate and intercessor in the defense of our salvation. It follows from this that if any one wishes to condemn us, he not only renders void the death of Christ, but also fights against the incomparable power with which the Father has honored Him, and with such power conferred on Him supreme authority. This great security which dares to triumph over the devil, death, sin and the gates of hell, ought to be deeply implanted in all godly hearts, for our faith is nothing unless we are persuaded for certain that Christ is ours, and that the Father is propitious to us in Him. There is, therefore, no more pernicious or destructive conception than the scholastic dogma of the uncertainty of salvation . . . *Who maketh intercession for us*. Paul required to make this explicit addition, to prevent the divine Majesty of Christ from terrifying us. Although, therefore, Christ holds

> all things in subjection under His feet from His lofty throne, Paul represents Him as a Mediator, whose presence it would be absurd for us to dread, since He not only invites us to Himself in a kindly manner, but also appears for us before the Father as Intercessor. We are not to measure this intercession by our carnal judgment, for we must not think of Him as humbly supplicating the Father on bended knee and with outstretched hands. Christ, however, is justly said to intercede for us, because He appears continually before the Father in His death and resurrection, which takes the place of eternal intercession, and to have the efficacy of lively prayer for reconciling the Father and making Him ready to listen to us (Calvin 1961, 185-86).

In this very citation, it becomes clear that in Calvin's view, Christ, at the right hand of the Father, is the perpetual mediator. He continually appears before the Father in his death and resurrection, but is simultaneously at the right hand of the Father—the one who obtained dominion over heaven and earth, and full of power and rules over all things. It is important to see Christ in Calvin's view in his mediatorship as the kingly priest. The prophetship of Christ is de-emphasized in the Calvinian view because its function is allotted to Scripture as the inscripturated Christ, Christ clothed with words which has to be rightly understood and expounded (Calvin 1961, 269).

According to Calvin, there had to be an exchange or buffering between Christ and us. Jesus Christ had to become Son of man in order that we could become children of God. If we had to ask Calvin, "In which nature did he [Christ] destroy death and sin?" he would say, "In His [Christ's] human nature!" That is how he could appease the Father's righteous indignation. Christ came primarily and most importantly to be our mediator and a sacrifice to appease the Father on our behalf (Kerr 1989, 72-72).

In Calvin's approach, Christ "ascended to heaven to fill all things" and thus truly inaugurated his kingdom at his ascension. Therefore, what Calvin perceives in the ascension is that Christ does ascend not for himself, but for us as the priestly king. The following titles, according to Kerr (1989, 79-80), in Calvin's view are part of Christ as the ascended one who fills all things:

- Ruler—who will rule with us; as our
- Head—who will gather us; as our
- Advocate—who will defend us; as our
- Intercessor—who intercedes for us; as our
- Redeemer—who redeems us; as our
- Promise—who promises eternal Salvation to us; and as our
- Judge—who judges us.

In Calvin's view, in Christ, we see the ultimate essence of every one of us, and of everything that is in Christ, we have glorious victory, reign, assurance, and eternal life.

One of the biggest points of contestation in the Calvinist tradition is whether the character of atonement and reconciliation in Christ is of a limited or unlimited nature. It suffices here to point to the notion of limited atonement in Calvin, as illustrated by Edwin Palmer in his book *The Five Points of Calvinism* (1980, 41-42). Palmer contrasts the Arminian stance of "universal atonement" against that of Calvin's "limited atonement." With reference to the Arminians, Calvin says that they propagate that Christ died for the entire world, with Judas and Esau included. This belief, Palmer eludes, makes a disjunction between what Christ did [he died for all] and what Christ accomplished [all are not saved]. He continues to argue that, for the Arminians, salvation is a "grab bag," that is, there is a package for all; however, some will grab one and some will not.

He moves on to say that they believe that Christ did not just shed his blood, but that he spilled it also. Thus, in terms of Calvin's views, the Arminians believed that Christ intended to save all in sincerity, yet in reality only "some will be saved." Hence, some of his blood "was wasted," for it was spilled (1980, 41). Palmer also elaborates, through another example, that the Arminians are like a man who more than a century ago was sentenced to be hanged, but who [that man] received the president's pardon, only to refuse it. In essence, what Palmer seeks to prove through this example is that if the Arminians' view is that while Christ's death may offer forgiveness, the sinner may still reject the forgiveness.

Palmer refers to the Calvinist's case of limited atonement, and he says Calvinists believe that Christ intended that he atone only for the ones his Father has given to him. The text they hold on to is John 6:37-40. Palmer continues to say that Calvin argued that if everyone's sins were paid for, then everyone would go to heaven. The reality is that not all people will be saved. According to Palmer, the texts that Calvin used to justify his view that only a limited number of people receive Christ's atonement are Matthew 1:21, which speaks about "His people;" John 10:15 and John 10:26, which refer to "His friends;" John 15:13 "His sheep;" and Ephesians 5:25, which speaks about "the bride." Some Calvinists, in a clearer expression of Calvin's pattern of reflection, have preferred the terms "definite or particular," instead of the term "limited" atonement. However, in a similar sense as Calvin, they "stress that the atonement which is unlimited in its power, is limited to a definite, particular number of people, namely the believers" (Palmer 1980, 42).

We must mention that in spite of the above statement, we should be aware of the theological debate on whether Calvin fully believed in his teaching of limited atonement or not. Paul van Buren's doctoral dissertation, *Christ in Our Place*, indicates Calvin's failure to recognize the notion of universal atonement, where the obvious line of reflection would have been to acknowledge the notion of universal atonement in the context. He simply did this so as not to contradict his basic premise of limited atonement (Gamble 1992, 201).

In Calvin's *Institutes* of 1559 ([1989] 2001a, 61), he directs us to the type of righteousness that the individual believer has to consider. He says that it is "a heavenly tribunal." With that in mind, Calvin goes on to warn us of applying our inferior standards in order to measure God's perfect justice. Calling our attention to the judgment seat of God, Calvin admonished us to proceed into a mode of self-introspection. The great question that we should ask ourselves is, "How shall we answer the heavenly judge when He calls us to account?" Calvin further calls upon the individual believer to work and accept a concept of a judge that is from Scripture, not created and brought forward by our own devices ([1989] 2001a, 62).

His view of the judgment seat of God also involves the devil. He must have been referring to Zachariah 3, when he portrayed the devil as being appearing before God to accuse us before God. What will work or be of benefit for the believer during the judgment, according to him (Calvin), is "the true intent of the will." Hypocrisy, which leads to "ostentatious display," according to him, will be condemned by God.

Calvin's description and portrayal of God is usually that of an awesome, glorious God of inconceivable purity and holiness, who is brighter than the stars, the sun, whose holiness out-shines that of angels. Such a God does not need to be appeased by good works, and even if the believer's good works matched the requirements of the law, that would not change us to be in the right state to meet his righteousness. In his writings, Calvin repeatedly condemns man's boastful self-righteous arrogance and also warns against any form of pride from the individual believer before the judgment seat of God. Furthermore, in a typical reform style, Calvin holds that there is absolutely nothing that can commend us to God. Not an iota of our being or merit can be accounted or credited toward the righteousness of God. Even that perfect righteousness of God is not to be applied by us on ourselves; it is God who does that ([1989] 2001a, 62).

3.3.2 White's View of Christ as Perpetual Priestly Conqueror and as Mediator

Christ is understood by White to have been the mediator of human beings immediately after the fall. He was the only one in the entire universe who could mediate between God and fallen humanity. Here the two faces of God are being depicted. The identification of Christ is portrayed as that of an advocate, a broker on behalf of sinful humanity, before the face of an offended God! White writes:

> Before the Father, He pleaded on the sinner's behalf, while the host of heaven awaited the result with an intensity of interest that words cannot express. Long continued was that mysterious communing—for the fallen sons of men . . . from everlasting He was the Mediator of the covenant, the one by whom all nations of the earth, both Jews and Gentiles, if they accepted Him, were to be blessed (*Review and Herald*, April 5, 1906).

There exists a conspicuous paradox of God's persona. The Father appears more stern and there is a mood of wrath and impending vengeance from the visage of God. The façade of Christ is depicted as deeply sorrowful, emotionally hurt, tense, and heart rent that pleads on behalf of helpless transgresses against the absence of God. Herein is depicted an unfathomable mysterious tension within the Godhead.

In her writing about Christ's salvific and reconciliatory function for us as our substitute, she points out that when Christ took on the responsibility of being our substitute, he suffered immensely, and he had to suffer outside the boundaries of Jerusalem (White [1898] 1948a, 742). From insult to renewed insult, from mockery to mockery, twice tortured by the scourge, all that night there had been scene after scene of a character to try the soul of man to the uttermost. In spite of all his suffering, she opines that Christ did not fail.

He never uttered a word, save that which glorified God. His bodily suffering was so severe that his human nature could no longer endure: "Again the burden was laid upon him, and again he fell fainting to the ground."

In a well-known quotation, she draws the lines together from the cross to the full operational mission of Christ in the sanctuary:

> The intercession of Christ in man's behalf in the sanctuary above is as essential to the plan of salvation as was His death upon the cross. By His death He began that work which after His resurrection He ascended to complete in heaven (White [1888] 1990a, 498).

Hence, before the cleansing of the sanctuary can be affected, there must be an investigation of the heavenly records, since, according to her, is to be determined who the receiver of Christ's atonement will be. So in the great day of final atonement and investigative judgment, the only cases considered are those of the professed people of God. The judgment of the wicked is a distinct and separate work and takes place at a later period. This investigation is part of the work of judgment, which Christ is now engaged in prior to his Second Coming. Like the early steadfast Adventists saw it, she sees it in this manner:

- The sin offering pointed to Jesus;
- The High Priest represents the mediator, Christ;
- The scapegoat represents the devil, Satan, who is the originator of sin;
- The repented sinner's sin will be placed on Satan after it has been removed from the heavenly sanctuary by Christ, our mediator; and:

> As the scapegoat was to be removed from the congregation into the wilderness, even so will Satan be forever removed from the presence of the

> Almighty and his people, "in the final destruction of sin and sinners" (White 1884, 268).

In the ongoing and prolonged sanctuary ministry, the cross of Christ plays an enormous role. Staying with the ambience of the biblical historical timeline and with a great regard to the most victorious words by Christ on the cross, "It is finished," she reflexively expresses the following:

> It was the hour of the evening sacrifice. The lamb representing Christ had been brought to be slain. Clothed in his significant and beautiful dress, the Priest stood with lifted knife, as did Abraham when he was about to slay his son. With intense interest the people were looking on. But the earth trembles and quakes; for the Lord Himself draws near. With a rending noise the inner veil of the temple is torn from top to bottom by an unseen hand, throwing open to the gaze of the multitude a place once filled with the presence of God. In this place the Shekinah had dwelt . . . No one but the High Priest ever lifted the veil separating this apartment from the rest of the temple. He entered in once a year to make atonement for the sins of the people. But . . . the most holy place of the Sanctuary is no longer Sacred (White [1898] 1948a, 756).

The most holy place of the earthly sanctuary is no longer sacred since the typical lamb, as a victim, escaped from the typical priest's presence. The most awaited time in Christian history had come—type met antitype through the vicarious death of Jesus, the Son of God.

Regarding the "once and for all" and "ongoing" effectuation of the death on the cross, the following points of White's approach can be summarized:

- The most prized sacrifice had been offered;
- Our access to God had been laid;

- A new dynamic way for the believer exists;
- There is direct access to God's forgiveness;
- Christ has earned the right to advocate on our behalf; and:

> There is no longer a need to offer animal sacrifices, since Christ has offered himself once and for always (White [1898] 1948a, 756-757).

In an even more ongoing way, the resurrection of Christ is a decisive part within the sanctuary ministry in the most prolonged and incisive way possible. She then moves us from the cross and takes us to the tomb where Jesus had been laid. When writing about the resurrection—we can almost hear the sounds of a triumphant trumpet—as White opens the portals of the grave:

> He is not in Joseph's new tomb; He is risen from the dead and ascended on high as Substitute and Surety for every believing soul (White 1979, 107).

From this scene, we are led to experience a sense of a glorious and awe-inspiring power, especially in the opening up and material presentation of Christ in his resurrection as substitute and surety for every believing soul. In actual fact, it is here where we are introduced to an added dimension of Christ's mission within the embracing ambience of the sanctuary ministry. White says Christ's death emphasizes the reality that Christ completed his mission on earth. In other words, had Christ failed to be obedient to God to the end of his life, before his death on the cross of Golgotha, it arises from the sense-making logic of the sanctuary ministry that Christ would not have arisen from the tomb. But having succeeded in accomplishing his work through perfect obedience to God, and persevering through the most painful, humiliating death, Christ conquered the power of death. Therefore, in

White's view, the just and proportionate requirements of death that Jesus met on behalf of the sinners of the world is vindicated, empowered, and affirmed "as substitute and surety for every believing soul" through his resurrection that is set forth in the next phase in the most holy place.

In the ongoing and perpetual sanctuary ministry, the ascension of Christ is that of one who is a divine conqueror. The name "divine conqueror," used for Christ's ascension into heaven, is an interesting alternate Christological title that White employed for Christ. In addition to the title of divine conqueror, is that Christ had, by his resurrection, "authenticated Himself as a living Savior." In this self-authentication of Christ, a glorifying majesty and empowering affirmation took place that is ongoing in the processual interceding of the priestly prophet, who as the resurrected can no longer be associated with death, but rather with his glorification within the heavenly cosmos.

When we move our eyes and transpose to Christ's Second Coming, White portrays Christ as ascending from Mount Olives, to which, in White's view, he shall return. Interestingly, White has another Christological title for Christ for the phase of his return: the Triumphant King. Christ who ascended into heaven is "in the form of humanity." His return will be in a similar manner with distinct differences. A major difference is that when Jesus returns, he will not co-descend in humility, as he has been while on earth in his first advent. On the contrary, he will come with divine glory, which he always had throughout eternity:

> Between the First and the Second Advent of Christ, a wonderful contrast will be seen. No human language can portray the scenes of the Second Coming of the Son of man in the clouds of heaven. He is to come with His own glory, and with the glory of the Father and of the holy angels. He will come clad in the robe of light, which He has worn from the days of eternity. Angels

> will accompany Him. Ten thousand times ten thousand will escort Him on His way (White 1988, 373).

Now, that is a depiction of his Second Coming. Regarding his ascension, prior to the Second Coming, White (1958b, 305) has the view that Christ took with him a host of redeemed people that he liberated on the day of his resurrection:

> After His resurrection, Christ did not show Himself to any save His followers; but testimony in regard to His resurrection was not wanting. Those who were raised with Christ "appeared unto many" (Matt. 27:53), declaring, "Christ has risen from the dead, and we are risen with Him." They bore testimony in the city to the fulfillment of the scripture, "Thy dead men shall live, together with my dead body shall they arise. Awake and sing, ye that dwell in dust: for thy dew is as the dew of herbs, and the earth shall cast out the dead" (Isa. 26:19).

These people, who were resurrected with Christ after having appeared before many and having relived their lives, died again. Nevertheless, the same group, if they were faithful, will be a part of "the great multitude" who will be resurrected from their graves at Christ's Second Coming (1 Thessalonians 4:16; Revelation 7:9). Essentially, the throng that was resurrected with Christ from their graves was a representation of the people whom Jesus will redeem in his Second Advent to our world.

Furthermore, the purpose of Jesus' resurrection and ascension is made plain to us by White when she exclaimed that Christ's ascension was for us, and that he lives for us and intercedes before our Father and our God on our behalf. She writes:

> The time had come for Christ to ascend to His Father's home. As a divine conqueror He was about

> to return with the trophies of victory to the heavenly courts. Before His death He had declared to His Father, "I have finished the work which Thou gavest Me to do" (John 17:4). After His resurrection He tarried on earth for a season, that His disciples might become familiar with Him in His risen and glorified body. Now He was ready for the leave-taking. He had authenticated the fact that He was a living Savior. His disciples need no longer associate Him with the tomb. They could think of Him as glorified before the heavenly universe (White [1898] 1948a, 829).

Hence, Jesus' identity is embellished with a vicarious role on behalf of God's dependent children, upon the self-denying and mediating, Son of God!

3.4 The Interactive Exchange of the Roles of Divinity and Humanity of Christ

3.4.1 Quiescent Divinity versus Active Divinity

So when did Jesus exercise his divine power? Why did he use his divine power? When did he function as human? The question may continue: If Jesus did engage his divine power while on earth, did he use his divine power in order to glorify himself? Did Jesus, at any time, zoom into his divinity in order that he might *alleviate* his suffering humanity? This questioning is vital, since it seeks to establish if White's view of Christ portrays a divinized human nature that was at a better advantage than that of the first Adam's sinless nature.

In order to illustrate this *interactional substantialism* position, we will be looking at various incidents that are recorded in the New Testament narratives through the eyes of White and Calvin. Let us first look at a portion of the narrative that relates to the storm on the Sea of Galilee, which Jesus calmed:

> When Jesus was awakened to meet the storm, He was at perfect peace. There was no trace of fear in word or look, for no fear was in His heart. But He rested not in the possession of almighty power. It was not as the "Master of earth and sky" that He reposed in quiet. That power He laid down, and He says, "I can of mine own self do nothing" (White [1898] 1948a, 336).

Through this passage, White intended to illustrate that Christ did not calm the stormy tempest of Galilee through the power of his divinity. Instead, as a human being like one of us, he calmed the storm through his absolute dependence on his heavenly Father. The first question was: "When did Jesus use his divine power?" We have already mentioned that White sometimes portrays Christ to be in a divine active mode, while at other times his divinity is in a quiescent mode, allowing more of his humanness to be revealed. Let us look at another example of Christ zooming into his divine active mode. Relating on Christ's triumphant entry, this is what White has to say:

> The glorious destiny that might have blessed Jerusalem had she accepted her Redeemer rose before the Son of God: He saw that she might through Him have been healed of her grievous malady, liberated from bondage, and established as the mighty metropolis of the earth . . . But the bright picture of what Jerusalem might have been fades from the Savior's sight (White [1898] 1948a, 577).

Although one may argue that prophets had the same visionary ability to see future events in panoramic vision, the fact that White states in this passage that Christ sees himself as Israel's Redeemer and that this picture "rose before the Son of God," seems to indicate that he was at that stage in his divine active mode. For only God can see himself as God! As a human being, he would see himself as dependent on God. Certainly, at this stage, Jesus did not merely speak as a mortal prophet. Had he been speaking in the same manner as that of other prophets, then White might have said that "the glorious destiny of Jerusalem, had she accepted her Redeemer, rose before the *Son of man*." Instead, she calls Him *Son of God*.

With regard to the Last Supper, White highlights another example of Christ's active divinity. Relating to Jesus and Judas, White wrote:

> By reading the secret purpose of the traitor's heart, Christ gave to Judas the final, convincing evidence of His divinity (White [1898] 1948a, 655).

Christ's divinity may be seen as active in yet another passage by White when she writes, regarding the Last Supper:

> Though He had humbled Himself of humanity, the Godhead was still His own. Christ alone could represent the Father to humanity, and this representation the disciples had been privileged to behold for over three years . . . Their faith might safely rest on the evidence given in Christ's works, works that no man, of himself, ever had done, or ever could do. Christ's work testified to His divinity . . . Christ was seeking to lead them from their low condition of faith to the experience they might receive if they truly realized what He was—God in human flesh (White [1898] 1948a, 655).

More remarkable about this passage are the words she wrote that followed:

> As Christ was speaking these words, the glory of God was shining from His countenance, and all present felt a sacred awe as they listened with rapt attention to His words (White [1898] 1948a, 655).

In order to answer the question as to why Jesus was in his active divinity mode, we may find the answer in the question, "Why was His divinity united with humanity?" White wrote:

> The Savior was deeply anxious for His disciples to understand for what purpose His divinity was united with humanity. He came to the world to display the glory of God, that man might be uplifted by its restoring power (White [1898] 1948a, 664).

From this passage, we are to learn that Christ's *active divinity* was for the revelation and glorification of God, so that mankind may be restored to God. It was not for his own glory that Christ had himself glorified through his divinity that was made manifest at random. We shall look at more examples in order to discover more of Christ's active divinity while he was in his human body, and to answer the question, "Did Christ have an advantage over the first Adam and did he use his divinity for show?"

According to White, as a child, Jesus did not engage his divinity in order to alleviate his chores. In fact, White purports that in all his stay in Nazareth, Jesus never made a show or display of his divinity (White [1898] 1948a, 74). However, writing about the time when Jesus' parents realized they had left him at the temple, when he was of adolescent age, White tells us of Jesus' response to his parents: "How is it that ye sought me?" Asked, the young Jesus:

> "Wist ye not that I must be about My Father's business?" And as they seemed not to understand His words, He pointed upwards! On His face was a light at which they wondered. Divinity was flashing through humanity (White [1898] 1948a, 81).

Here is demonstrated the combination of divinity and humanity in the one person of Jesus Christ. There is a manifestation of *interactional substantialism* at this point.

But for what purpose, we may ask, is this exchange between divinity and humanity?

It appears from the passage above, and those that followed, that the divinity of Christ became active so that Jesus' parents would better understand that they were privileged to be entrusted with the custody of the Son of the Highest God. This seems to be intentional, to remind the human parents of Jesus that even though it was natural for them to see and perceive him as their child, and therefore, treat him like natural parents treat their children, he was more than just an ordinary human child; he was also a divine Son of the Most High God.

As we follow the life of Christ and seek to understand his divine and human modes, let us now follow him to the time after he had been arrested and brought before Pontius Pilate. There is something about Christ's person that must have disturbed Pontius Pilate when we consider White's description of what happened at Pilate's court. White writes:

> In fear and self-condemnation Pilate looked upon the Savior. In the vast sea of upturned faces, His alone was peaceful. About His head a soft light seemed to shine. Pilate said in his heart, "He is God" (White [1898] 1948a, 739).

Here we see yet another manifestation of *interactional substantialism*. Jesus' divinity is being activated so that we see more of his divinity then of his humanity!

Another example where we see the *interactional substantialism* of Christ is at a site traditionally known by some as the Mount of Transfigurations. It is there that Jesus took along with him the three disciples who were to witness his agony at the Garden of Gethsemane. This is how White describes what transpired on that Mount:

> While He is bowed in lowliness upon the stony ground, suddenly the heavens open, the golden gates

> of the city of God are thrown wide, and holy radiance descends upon the Mount, enshrouding the Savior's form. Divinity from within flashes through humanity, and meets the glory coming from above . . . Christ stands in Godlike majesty (White [1898] 1948a, 421).

Should we ask White why Jesus' divinity became active or was manifested in this instance, White answers:

> Now the burden of His prayer is that they may be given a manifestation of the glory He had with the Father before the world was, that His kingdom may be revealed to human eyes and that they may witness a manifestation of His divinity that will comfort them in the hour of His supreme agony with the knowledge that He is of a surety the Son of God and that His shameful death is a part of the plan of redemption (White [1898] 1948a, 420-421).

It is clear from the above passage that Christ's divinity was manifested for specific reasons. Jesus allowed his divinity to manifest for the sake of the disciples. The disciples were to witness the revelation of God's glory and to believe that he truly was divine and that he was truly the Son of God. According to White, the manifestation of Jesus' divinity, that is, active divinity, had the following results:

- God and those with him in heaven were cognizant of the sins of the Jews, having rejected Jesus;
- Clear insight into the redeemer's work was displayed;
- Things beyond human comprehension were seen and heard;
- The disciples became eyewitnesses;
- The disciples realized the Messiah-ship of Christ; and:

> At that point, they knew that Jesus was acknowledged by the universe and by heaven itself (White [1898] 1948a, 425).

From White's writing, we know of another incident where the quiescent divinity of Christ became active divinity—at the cleansing of the Temple! In visionary language, White described what transpired and says:

> The confusion hushed. The sound of traffic and bargaining has ceased. The silence becomes painful. A sense of awe overpowers the assembly. It is as if they were arraigned before "the tribunal of God" to answer for their deeds. Looking upon Christ they behold divinity flash through the garb of humanity. The Majesty of heaven stands as the Judge, will stand at the last day . . . His form seems to rise above them in commanding dignity, and a divine light illuminates His countenance (White [1898] 1948a, 158).

Why is interactional substantialism important in White's approach? Rephrased, the question could be asked as to why, in this instance, did Christ manifest his divinity through his humanness? Stated differently: Why did Christ's quiescent divinity become active divinity at this moment? White's reply is clear when she states, "Jesus was announcing His mission as the Messiah" (White [1898] 1948a, 161). In another chapter where she comments on Christ's temptation, White mentions that Jesus was not to show or manifest his divinity for himself.

Neither here nor at any subsequent time in his earthly life did he work a miracle on his own behalf (White [1898] 1948a, 119).

3.4.2 Interactional Substantialism While Dying at Golgotha

White perceived the death of Christ on the cross of Golgotha as an indispensable necessity for the blending of the mercy and justice of God. Sin had caused such a gulf between the two that there appears to have been tension within the realm of the Godhead. White reflects in metaphors full of imaginative imagery of how God the redeemer expressed his justice and mercy in the cross, which is planted midway between heaven and earth:

> Justice and Mercy stood apart, in opposition to each other, separated by a wide gulf. The Lord our Redeemer clothed His divinity with humanity, and wrought out in behalf of man a character that was without spot or blemish. He planted His cross midway between heaven and earth, and made it the object of attraction, which reached both ways, drawing both Justice and Mercy across the gulf. Justice moved from its exalted throne, and with all the armies of heaven approached the cross. There it saw One equal with God bearing the penalty for all injustice and sin. With perfect satisfaction Justice bowed in reverence at the cross, saying, It is enough (White [1953] 1985, 469).

In a similar train of thought, she said at a different occasion:

> God bowed His head satisfied. Now justice and mercy could blend. Now He could be just, and yet be the Justifier of all who should believe on Christ. He [God] looked upon the victim expiring on the cross, and said, "It is finished. The human race shall have another trial" (White [1953] 1985, 470).

According to White, Jesus was still caring and compassionate about those around him, regardless of his sufferings. There were women at the scene of Christ's crucifixion who cried for Christ out of human sympathy. "Daughters of Jerusalem," he said, "Weep not for Me, but weep for yourselves, and for your children" (Luke 23:28). From the scene before him, Christ looked ahead to the time of the destruction of Jerusalem. "In that terrible scene, many of those who were weeping for Him were to perish with their children." In his divine-prophetic mode, Jesus was looking down the corridors of history from the time that Jerusalem was to fall to the time of the judgment of the world: "Then shall they begin to say to the mountains, Fall on us; and to the hills, cover us. For if they do these things in a green tree, what shall be done in the dry?" (White [1898] 1948a, 743).

Again, as earlier where reference was made to Christ's "quiescent nature," the notion of Jesus being in a state of interactional substantialism emerges. Even though there is no apparent visible light glowing through Christ, and White makes no mention that divinity was flashing through his humanity, there is a divine manifestation that is almost overlooked. That divine manifestation can be gleaned through the words of Christ when he said, "For if they do these things in a green tree, what shall be done in the dry?" Christ's reference of the green tree is a reference "to Himself, the Innocent Redeemer" (White [1898] 1948a, 743). Certainly, here is some form of tension of interaction between the dual natures of Christ. The point we should not lose sight of is that no human being can refer to himself or herself as "the Innocent Redeemer," unless he or she blasphemes. Having said that, we should concede that there must have been an activity within the dual natures of Christ at such a point. Christ, in his humanity, was moved by his divinity. There is a manifestation of interactional substantialism since in this prophetic utterance there is a personal recognition of himself as an "Innocent Redeemer." This is, by the way, yet another title for Christ regarding his identity.

3.4.2.1 Calvin on the Tension Between the Two Natures of Christ

One of the questions we posed in the previous chapters is how does Calvin perceive the unity of the two natures? The best illustration Calvin could use, as mentioned previously, was the formation of human beings. To Calvin, the body and soul could exist in one person "without confusion of substance," so was it possible for the two natures of Christ to co-exist in unity in one person? Calvin adamantly spoke out against an "either . . . or" continuum regarding the two natures of Christ. He says:

> Frantic and furious spirits fasten on the attributes of humanity to destroy his divinity; and on the other hand, on those of his divinity to destroy his humanity (Calvin [1989] 2001b, 418).

Calvin condemned Nestorius, whom he felt "dissected rather than distinguished between the two natures." He also condemned Eutyches and Michael Servetus of his time. Calvin was particularly against Servetus for denying that Christ was the Son of God, since he [Servetus] believed that Christ could not be a Son of God as he was begotten "in the womb of the Virgin." Calvin went on to defend the traditional stance of Chalcedon of the hypostatic union, which was a term used by people of old to refer to a person who was a composite of two natures.

Conspicuously, and similar to White's stance, we can see that there is tension in Calvin's Christology of the two natures. Hence, if we were to pose the question as to how he sees the text, which implicitly acknowledges Christ's subordination to God the Father?, Calvin would tell us that he sees no difficulty in the subordination of the humanity of Christ, as expressed in the various biblical texts, nor where Christ speaks of his eternal divinity. What he sees is expressed in what he calls "a figure of speech" used by people of old, "a communication of properties." In the discussion about the *alloiosis* earlier, it was pointed out that *alloiosis* refers to a linguistic operational tool of "a figure of speech which was used by Calvin and Zwingli to explain the ancient notion of a communication of properties:"

> Thus, also the Scriptures speak of Christ: they sometimes attribute to him what must be referred solely to his humanity, sometimes what belongs uniquely

> to his divinity; and sometimes what embraces both natures but fits neither alone. And they so earnestly express this union of the two natures that is in Christ as sometimes to interchange them. This figure of speech is called by the ancient writers "the communicating of properties" ([1559] 1960a, 4, 17, 12).

Where Calvin writes about the term "flesh" in John 1:14, "and the Word was made flesh" refers to Christ as the Son of God coming to put on our flesh and showing himself openly to the world. The evangelist John, according to Calvin, touches briefly upon the ineffable mystery that the Son of God put on human nature. Even though brief, he is astonishingly clear:

> At this point, some mad people amuse themselves with frivolous subtleties and make fools of themselves. They say, "The Word is said to have been made flesh" in the sense that God conceived the Son in his own mind, and then sent him into the world as a man; as though the Word were I do not know what sort of shadowy image, But we have shown that the statement refers to a real hypostasis in the essence of God.
>
> By saying "flesh," the writer expresses himself more forcibly than if he had said, "*He was made man*." He means to state that the Son of God, for our sake, left the height of his heavenly glory and humbled himself to a state at once low and abject . . . Flesh here means not, as so of the with Paul, our nature corrupt by sin but mortal men in general . . . At the same time, however, we must notice that this is a figure of speech: [flesh] which is one part of man, stands for him as a whole. Therefore, Apollinaris was foolish to fancy that Christ put on a human body without the soul. (Calvin 1958, 163).

In the last sentence of the quotation, Calvin refers to Apollinaris (d. 392) who taught that Christ had a human body and the life of a man, but that in him, his rational soul and conscious mind as the divine *logos* is the animating principle permeating and determining the human bodily flesh. Thus, he represented Christ as neither God nor man but as a perfect, mainly bodily, human being so animated and permeated by his divinity that there was no room for his human self-consciousness. He was repudiated and condemned in the fourth century, but orthodoxy was permanently influenced by him (Harnack 1961, 149-159). Therefore, Calvin, in his version of the interactional substantialist approach, operates very strongly with a figure of speech, or the *alloiosis*, in which the humanity of Christ refers simultaneously to his divinity in the sense of a similarity between the distinctive existence of both humanity and divinity.

The notion of *alloiosis* is definitely not carried by a formal syllogistic mode of the sameness of the substances of the divinity and humanity in which one part is fused with the other to acquire the substantive properties of the other, as in the view of Apollinaris. Appollinaris' views go in two directions. On one hand, his view that the divine substance permeates the human substance in Christ influenced all the permeation schemes in history, including that of the Lutheran tradition. On the other hand, his view that Christ's humanity is totally enveloped, embodied, and transformed by his divinity influenced the schemes in which Christ appears as a divinized and sacramentalized human being, including that of the orthodox Roman Catholic view in operation in church and ecclesial practice (Harnack 1961, 151).

Breen, in an essay, titled, "John Calvin and the Rhetorical Tradition" (1968, 122-123), shows that Calvin's approach is effectuated through a rhetorical syllogistic style of enthymeme, comprised of two members, that differs from the known formalistic syllogism style, comprised of three members, such as a *major premise: All men are mortal; minor premise: Socrates is a man; and conclusion: therefore, Socrates is mortal.* A syllogistic enthymeme could read as follows: *Major premise: all men are mortal*; *conclusion:*

therefore, Socrates is mortal. The sense-making veracity of the meaning of the connection of different words within a rhetorical oratorical setting is more important than the truth that emerges by comparison of the substances of the parts connected. The *alloiosis* notion is born from the Renaissance rhetorical tradition, especially through the way Cicero has been delivered in the Renaissance. The notion of *alloiosis* in a different sense than Aristotle's syllogistic logic is a tailor-made linguistic tool for Calvin and Zwingli to fit the bill of the similarities between the divine and human natures of Christ.

What this means is that it is congruous to speak of Christ's divinity and humanity through similarities in which one part of Christ stands for the whole Christ, such as for Christ to speak of himself of his human weakness and his limited knowledge, as well as we can interchangeably speak of his divine attributes. Examples of these can be seen in John 8:58, when Christ said, "Before Abraham was I AM." Christ could also say he does not know when the last day will be, and where the Scripture says, "He increased in wisdom and in stature." Since divinity cannot be prone while still on earth to these human weaknesses and limitations while as a human being he was, he could rightly and interchangeably be called either way.

In fact, Calvin moves on to point out an interesting point—that is, there are texts that refer to both his duel attributes simultaneously. These, according to Calvin, we find especially in the Gospel book of John. An example that Calvin implies is found in 1 Corinthians 2:8, where it is mentioned that the Jews crucified the Lord. Another text used is Acts 20:28, which says "that God purchased the Church with His blood." These texts demonstrate what Calvin calls a communication of properties, but then clearly understood in the *alloiosis*, or enthymeme sense, of the word (Calvin [1989] 2001b, 416-417).

One question that keeps prodding one's mind is: Since Calvin perceives that the miraculous condescension of

Christ did not mean that he "abandoned" heaven, for he was still omnipresent in heaven as well, what are the implications regarding his Sonship in which Christ is engaged? What happens to the aspect of his voluntary subordination, and rightfully so, his humanity? Calvin, in discussing the words of Jesus according to John 12—"Now, my soul is troubled, and what shall I say?"—points to the preceding discourse of Jesus in which he exhorted his disciples to deal with death:

> There he [Jesus] showed more than heroic courage in exhorting his disciples not only to undergo death, but to face it willingly and eagerly whenever needful. But now he shrinks from death and seems to go soft. However, here we do not read anything that does not agree with the believers' own experience. If scoffers laugh at this, it is no wonder; one cannot understand it except by experience.
>
> Besides, it was necessary for our salvation that the Son of God should have been affected in this way. In his death, we must first consider the work of expiation, which appeased the wrath and curse of God; this he certainly could not have done unless our sin had been transferred to him. The death, therefore, to which he was subjected had to be dreadful even to him, because he could not have made satisfaction for us unless he had known God's dreadful judgment. We know better the enormity of sin because the Heavenly Father exacted such a dire punishment of his only begotten Son. Therefore, we must realize that death was not a pleasure or a game for Christ, and that he suffered excruciation to the utmost for our sakes.
>
> And it was not absurd that the Son of God should have been thus troubled. In the act of expiation, the secret divinity of the Son was quiescent and did not exercise its power. Christ in fact put on not only

> our flesh but also our human feeling; and this he did voluntarily. He was afraid not by constraint, but because he willingly subjected himself to fear. It must be firmly held that his fear was real and not fictitious. But he was unlike the rest of mankind in that, as we have said elsewhere, his feelings were tempered by obedience to the righteous God.
>
> Christ's humanity in feeling has a further value for us. If Christ had not been troubled by the fear of death, which of us would take his example seriously? It is not given to us that we should face death without a troubled mind; so, when we hear that he was not made of iron, we gather our forces and set out to follow him; and the weakness of our flesh which troubles us at death does not hinder us from joining our Leader in battle (Calvin 1958, 163-164).

Interestingly, in this quotation, Calvin asserts that it is absurd that the Son of God, who is closely connected to Jesus, should have been troubled as Jesus had been troubled as human being and that thus the secret divinity of the Son was quiescent and did not exercise its power in the act of expiation. This whole reflexive train of thought is typical of Calvin regarding the humanity and divinity of Christ. Sometimes the divinity comes more to the fore and sometimes the humanity. In this particular event of Jesus being troubled, it is more the human side of Christ that is coming to the fore in Calvin's close correlation between Christ voluntarily putting on our flesh and our human feelings and the value for us of Christ's humanity in feeling.

The question may be asked whether there will be a cessation of Christ's subordination to his Father later, sometime in the future, or will Christ retain his subordination forever? In 1 Corinthians 15:24, we read that, at the end, Christ will deliver the kingdom of God to the Father, and in Philippians 2:8, we read that Christ was given the scepter of royalty and was obedient to the Father, and subjected himself to the lowest point possible, and was then glorified by the Father. What will happen to Christ's act of subordination? Calvin responds by saying that the act of Christ's subordination to the Father "is only for a time, until we enjoy the immediate presence of his Godhead" (Calvin [1989] 2001b, 417).

The answer as to what happens to Christ's humanity and subordination to God the Father is perhaps best seen from Calvin's perspective in his following words:

> Let us, therefore, regard it as the key of true interpretation, that those things, which refer to the office of Mediator are not spoken of the divine or human nature simply. Christ therefore shall reign until He appears to judge the world, in as much as, according to the measure of our feeble capacity, He now connects us with the Father . . . then Christ, having accomplished the office of Mediator, shall cease to be the vice-regent of the Father, and will be content with the glory which He possessed before the world was (Calvin [1989] 2001b, 418).

Calvin further states that "God will then cease to be the head of Christ, and Christ's own Godhead will then shine forth of itself, whereas it is now in a manner veiled" (Calvin [1948] 2001b, 418). The purpose and use of Christ's priestly office is that of "a pure stainless Mediator. He is by His holiness to reconcile us to God." God's righteousness prevents us from having direct access to him, according to Calvin. He goes as far as portraying a grim picture of an angry judge who is angry with us. Hence, Christ the priest, knowing that a ransom ought to be sacrificed in order to appease the wrath of God, fills that office, says Calvin. But how? Through his vicarious sacrifice, his death is the answer. We ourselves become priests in Christ and have access to God in his sanctuary with our sacrifices, prayers, and praises. Through Christ's priesthood, we:

- Are reconciled to God;

- We have a ransom in Christ; and
- We have access to God as priests before him (Kerr 1989, 75-77).

Calvin's view about Christ being our mediator is that even though the sinner's condition may have been without stain, he or she would still be unworthy and incapable of aspiring to the presence of God (Porter and Greengrass 1983, 26).

One has to be constantly aware that Calvin sees Christ in his office and capacity as mediator as perpetually moving to and fro through nearly the whole biblical historical timeline up to the stage at the end where, in Calvin's view, Christ's mediatorship comes to an end. In the words of Calvin above, *then Christ, having accomplished the office of mediator, shall cease to be the vice-regent of the Father and will be content with the glory that he possessed before the world was.* In what follows in the next section, the identity of Christ is discussed through inquiring about his salvific work and the offices and titles he held and acquired, since all of these offices and titles have to do with his identity. This leads us to our next topic, which deals with the offices of Christ.

3.4.2.2 White on the Tension Between Divinity and Humanity

Regarding his divine manifestation, White states that Christ bore testimony of his divinity in the way he died (White [1898] 1948a, 751). Yet there is a paradoxical statement that she makes regarding his divinity:

> The withdrawal of the divine countenance from the Savior in this hour of supreme anguish pierced his heart . . . so great was this agony that his physical pain was hardly felt (White [1898] 1948a, 753).

This appears to be a reversal of the permeation paradigm in Lutheran approaches in which Christ divinity permeates his humanity. The withdrawal of Christ's divinity from his humanity is a very good example of White's interactional substantialism, in which she could take up a position in her divine historical reflexive world from above as divinely enacted, from below as through Christ's humanity enacted, and from the side as the perspective in which Christ, as mediator to human beings, is midway between heaven and earth.

One has to raise a question: Regarding White's description of the withdrawal of divinity, which part of divinity is White referring to? Is the divine withdrawal that of his Father, who was with him from eternity, or is the divine withdrawal that of his own quiescent divinity, which he still had with his human nature? At times, it may appear as though she refers to the divine withdrawal of the Father. The ambiguity comes through a statement she makes a few lines later: "God and his holy angels were beside the cross. The Father was with His Son. Yet His persona was not revealed." The Son's agony as human is further explained in the following statement, "In the thick darkness, God veiled the last human agony of His Son." White asserts that Christ in his dying moment after uttering the words, "It is finished . . ." Christ's face shone with a glory as that of "the sun" (White [1898] 1948a, 754-756). The element of White's Christological operational active movement of interactional substantialism comes in these sentences strongly to the fore.

At this junction, it is fitting that we make a transition to a perception of the complex and diversified person of Christ. We mentioned in our second problem-setting that the notion of transformational trans-substantialism is mainly the everyday Roman Catholic sacramentalist position, operating in Catholic rituals and religious practice, in which Christ is experienced as a divine sacred and sacramentalized human being who is simultaneously the pre-existent deity and Son of God. We should look at as to what extent are there trans-substantialist fragments and snippets, as well as of the con-substantialist position in which the humanity is permeated by the divinity to be found in White's and Calvin's approaches.

3.5 Titles, Offices and Dimensions of Christ's Identity

3.5.1 Calvin's View of Christ's Multidimensionality

The contextual traditional formula of many Reformers during Calvin's era of Christ's offices was that of a twofold one of priest and the other of king. Calvin went to great lengths to develop the *munus triplex*, or the notion of the triple offices of Christ into a triple formula of priest, king, and prophet. However, Calvin cannot be attributed to be the first proponent of the triple offices in the era of the sixteenth-century Reformation. One of the first Reformers to suggest a threefold office was Osiander, while Bucer in his *Enarrationes in Evangelica* in 1536, stated clearly the combination of the three offices of Christ:

> *Rex regum Christus est, summus sacerdos, et prophetarum caput* (quoted in Battles 1969, 495).

It is probably more appropriate to say that the traditional formula owes its wide acclamation to Calvin's use of it in central parts of his writings on Christ's mediatorship and salvific meaning. Notwithstanding the theological criticism of Ritschl and Ernesti, Calvin's formula of triple offices found its way into the convictions of theologians such as Brunner, Schleiermacher, Gerhard, Bavinck, and Neuman, and even transcended into the ranks of Anglican, Lutheran, and Catholic theology (Jansen 1956, 16-36).

There were two types of criticisms of the triple office formula: One was represented by those who, like Ernesti, wanted to reform Luther's priest-king formula; the other, like Ritschl, who objected to the notion of "office," rather preferred a concept of love over a concept of law (Jansen 1956, 16-36).

It should not be surprising that the seventeenth-century Reformed Orthodoxy, through its embrace of the triple office, had experienced an abundance of exegetical illuminations and the production of an amazing number of biblical analogies that transcend the limited realms of a dynamic view of Christ's identity. Jansen said it well in his reference to nineteenth-century liberal theology:

> The Jesus of Ritschl and Harnack was clad in prophetic garments but was stripped of his Kingly and Priestly vestments (Jansen 1956, 20).

Having said this, it is perhaps suitable to admit that even though the triplex of priest, king, and prophet formula is a more wholesome form of Christ's work and person, it still does not fully describe the complete person of Christ. Many examples were drawn from the biblical historical timeline and set in correlation with people's sense-making views of their local context and era to underscore the notion of the triplex office as a truly biblical view. Examples of such were that human beings were created in three spheres—a *heart* that loves God, a *hand* that rules in his stead, and a *mind* that knows him. When human beings sinned, they lost their triune dignity. Hence, the Messiah condescended and became the *Second Adam* who ensured our salvation, and through his unfaltering *obedience* as priest, king, and prophet, the lost Edenic status of humankind was procured and restored. Not only did this triple doctrine seek to permeate the study of man's salvation, but it sought to explore the avenues of the triune God. It stated that Christ obtained the kingdom from his *Father* through the Holy Ghost. He functioned as prophet (Jansen 1956, 17).

The contribution it has made in theological schools, churches, and institutions, and in the lives of many people in their experience of religious faith, is that of laying a foundation for an open and increased list of the various facets of Christ's extensive multifaceted identity springing forth from Scripture. This does not mean that there were no other perceptions of his identity based on Christ's work being propagated at the time. However, a better understanding of the nature of human beings and the work of Christ was achieved through the formula of the triple offices, which was combined and fused from an array of reflexive attributes from the whole biblical historical timeline as the exploration area from where titles, attributes, and offices of Christ had been collected and gathered.

The name Christ, according to Calvin, refers to those three offices, since priests, prophets, and kings were anointed with holy oil. Furthermore, Calvin states that the Messianic name was attributed to the mediator, who was named in his office of kingship. This person, says Calvin, was anointed for the purpose of witnessing and proclaiming God's grace in a way different from those in a similar office. Calvin gets a little involved and says that this anointing, which he received to become a "teacher," is not for his own interest, but for the entire body. When he would come, he would put an end to all prophecies. For Calvin, Christ is mainly to be seen as God's inscripturated embodiment as prophet in Scripture. As a figure of speech, the words of the Bible act as the clothes for Christ. In regard to the meaning of the word "prophecy," Calvin in his commentary of Romans 12:4-8, says he prefers:

> To follow those who understand the word in the wider sense to mean the peculiar gift of revelation by which a man performs the office of interpreter with skill and dexterity in expounding the will of God. In the Christian Church, therefore, prophecy at the present day is simply the right understanding of Scripture, and the particular gift of expounding it, since all the ancient prophecies and all the oracles of God have been concluded in Christ and his Gospel (Calvin 1961, 269).

With regard to his kingship, Calvin would have his readers understand that Christ's kingship is for our benefit. But this benefit is far superior to the benefits that can be enjoyed in the earthly life; they are spiritual (Calvin [1989] 2001b, 429). According to Calvin, the function of Christ is mainly to his office of kingship. This kingship, being of a spiritual dimension, has benefits for the individual believer:

- Through it we are raised to eternal life;
- We are enriched with salvation;
- We are conquerors against evil forces;
- We are taught endurance;
- We are inspired and triumphant; and
- We are fortified and loved (Calvin [1989] 2001b, 427-431).

3.5.2 White's View of Christ Multidimensional Ministering

With regard to Christ's earthly ministry, White portrays a messiah who cared and ministered to the needs of humanity. She points out that it was for this reason that Christ came to live among humans—to reveal God's infinite love. She states that Christ described his earthly mission when he said:

> The Lord hath anointed Me to preach the Gospel to the poor; He hath sent Me to heal the broken-hearted, to preach deliverance to the captives, and recovering of sight to the blind, to set at liberty them that are bruised (White [1893] 1982, 11).

By unwrapping the aspects of White's passage, one could distinguish at least five dimensions of Christ's identity. Thus, he is:

- Christ, the Preacher—"The Lord . . . to preach . . ."
- Christ, the Healer—"to heal the broken-hearted . . ."
- Christ, the Liberator—"to set at liberty them that are bruised . . ."
- Christ, the Deliverer—"to preach deliverance to the captives . . ."
- Christ, the Revelator of God's glory—"and recovery of sight to the blind."

The question worth posing at this juncture is whether Christ's identity blended with his work while he was on earth? According to White, Jesus fulfilled what he professed. He went about healing the sick, and in fact some "whole villages" were completely cleansed of diseases as Christ passed by them. He revealed mercy, love, and compassion. His heart was full of the greatest mercy and even children were attracted to him. His work, White says, was evidence "of His divine anointing" (White [1893] 1982, 11).

How did Christ describe his own identity? What kind of man was he? According to White, people of all ranks were attracted to him. He spoke in love and in truth. He never spoke carelessly and he was never rude. When he would speak out against hypocrisy and sin, there were tears in his voice. Even those who rejected him were regarded with tender pity. His entire life was one of caring for others. He exercised self-denial. Everyone was special to him. He saw every soul as his mission to save. According to White, all streams of love and compassion streamed from the Father's heart and were manifested in Jesus Christ, and were ultimately passed on to the sons and daughters of Adam and Eve. It was for our sakes that Christ became a sorrower (White [1898] 1948a, 12-13).

To White, the eternal Christ is the thought of God made audible (White [1898] 1948a, 20). To various offices that describe his identity, another office could be added and that is of teacher or prophet. Regarding Christ's ministry, White writes:

> So in the heavenly courts, in His ministry for all created beings; through the beloved Son, the Father's life flows out to all; through the Son, it returns, in praise and joyous service, a tide of love, to the great Source of all. And thus through Christ the circuit of beneficence is complete, representing the character of the great Giver, the law of life (White [1898] 1948a, 21).

This is the picture of his work, even before he came to earth to be born of mankind. Christ was the only being who could enter into all the counsels of God. It was through Christ that God created all the heavenly beings. It is clear from the above that Christ's work, even before sin entered heaven, was that of the mediator—heaven's commander—and the "sovereign of heaven, one in power and authority with the Father" (White [1888] 1990a, 494-495). For this study, it is important to notice the title names of Christ that we find in White's writings. In many of White's passages, it is clear that Christ is a medium of God's act of creation, which results in various parts of White's writings identifying Christ as mediator, king, teacher, and prophet.

White repeatedly mentions that Christ came to manifest the glory of God to this world. He brought his glorious light to this dark, sinful world. His dwelling with humankind was intended to reveal God to both angels and men. Jesus veiled himself with the garb of humanity so that he may bring light to a dark world. His attempt to tabernacle with humankind, according to White, varied from the burning bush, which had been chosen by the deity as a representation to the cloudy pillar by day and a pillar of light by night, in which God, in his humble way, could communicate his will to human beings. Hence, through a humble human form, Christ came to dwell with humankind in order to teach us about his divine character (White [1898]1948a, 23).

Furthermore, the great contribution that White has made to the entire group of mainline churches is one of her fundamental operational doctrines in which Christ is dynamically being portrayed as a perpetual intercessor:

> In the service of the Jewish priesthood, we are continually reminded of the sacrifice and intercession of Christ. All who come to Christ today are to remember that His merit is the incense that mingles with the prayers of those who repent of their sins and receive pardon and mercy and grace. Our need of Christ's intercession is constant (White [1953] 1985, 482-483).

White's view with regard to the heavenly courts and the judicial procedure is that, unlike most of the earthly courts, the advocate and judge of the human race is the same as the one who represents heaven on behalf of the triune God. Another interesting view presented to us by White is that there is no "*appeals court*" in heaven. Should the human soul be found guilty and sentenced to eternal damnation, that soul cannot appeal to the Father or the Holy Spirit because all judgment setting and final decision making rests with the *Son of man*. The decision is final. The reason why God has committed all judgment and the entire judicial process in heaven to Christ is based on the undergirding premise that Christ is both human and divine, and that heaven and earth are connected in Christ. Hence, no better being in the universe is more suited then the *Son of man*. In this we are again presented with the underlying synthesis of our theme of this book—that Christ is centrally and actively positioned in the midst of God's grand acts of creation, reconciliation, renewal, and fulfillment. Christ is not only centrally engaged in God's act of creation of human beings and the natural cosmic world, but Christ is central to the entire alphabet of the *science of salvation* in which Christ is both mediator and judge. In the following passage, White explains why Christ is both mediator and judge:

> By personal experience Christ is acquainted with the warfare which, since Adam's fall, has been constantly going on. How appropriate, then, for Him to be the judge. *To Jesus, the Son of man, is committed all judgment. There is one mediator between God and men. Only by Him can we enter the kingdom of heaven.* He is the Way, the Truth, and the Life. *From His decision there is no appeal.* He is the Rock of ages, a rock rent on purpose that every tried, tempted soul may find a sure hiding place. "The Father judgeth no man, but hath committed all judgment unto the Son." "He hath given him authority to execute

> judgment also because he is the Son of man." *In His superadded humanity consist the reason of Christ's appointment. God has committed all judgment unto the Son, for without controversy He is God manifest in the flesh.* God designed that the Prince of sufferers in humanity should be judge of the whole world. He who came from the heavenly courts to save man from eternal death; He whom men despised, rejected, and upon whom they heaped all the contempt of which human beings, inspired by Satan, are capable; He who submitted to be arraigned before an earthly tribunal, and who suffered the ignominious death of the cross—He alone is to pronounce the sentence of reward or of punishment. He who submitted to the suffering and humiliation of the cross here, in the counsel of God is to have the fullest compensation, and ascend the throne acknowledged by all the heavenly universe as the King of saints. He has undertaken the work of salvation, and shown before unfallen worlds and the heavenly family that the work He has begun He is able to complete . . . In that day of final punishment and reward, both saints and sinners will recognize in Him who was crucified the Judge of all living (White [1953] 1985, 483).

To the offices that describe his interactional identity, White adds yet another office and that is of teacher or prophet. As a teacher, he would teach God's people the deep things of God, and as a prophet, he would mediate between divinity and humanity in predicting the future. Hence, through a humble human form, Christ came to dwell with humanity in order to teach us about his divine character (White [1898] 1948a, 23).

In many instances, White writes of the substitutionary work of Christ. She believed that Christ's duel natures qualify him to be our substitute and surety. His possession of all the divine attributes and his perfect humanity guaranteed him as our surety and substitute. The substitution and surety that she refers to is a direct and explicit reference to Christ's vicarious death. Jesus made "a voluntary sacrifice" when he gave back the scepter into the Father's hand and chose to condescend lower than the angelic host and lower than the royalties of humanity, allowing himself to suffer a substitutionary vicarious death (White [1898] 1948a, 22-23).

When Christ took on a human form, Christ identified himself mediatorially with the title of priest. Writing about Christ as the priest who is himself the victim, White cited:

> So Christ took the form of a servant, and offered sacrifice, Himself a Priest, Himself the victim. He was wounded for our transgressions; He was bruised for our iniquities . . ." (White [1898] 1948a: 25).

In another passage, she refers to Christ as the offer and the offering:

> Christ is bearing a double position of offer and offering (White [1953] 1985, 463).

White's approach to Christ as priest bearing the dual entitlement of being the offered victim for all and the priest executing the priestly function is that Christ is right now our intercessor in the heavenly sanctuary. At the same time, Christ, through his sacrifice and work of mediation, is both builder and the foundation of the Church. Speaking in a wonderfully mixed metaphor of a heavenly priest on a throne, she writes:

> He shall sit and rule upon His throne; and He shall be a Priest upon His throne: As a Priest, Christ is now set down with the Father in His throne (White [1888] 1990a, 41).

Her mixed metaphor of a heavenly priest on a throne is an inter-linkage with many of the titles that Christ carries. By centrally positioning Christ as the perpetual prophetly priest as mediating intercessor in the heavenly sanctuary, White inter-links Jesus' prophetly priesthood as mediator with him being heavenly commander.

3.6 The Second Coming of Christ

3.6.1 Calvin's Scriptural Exclusivity of Prophecy on the Second Coming

Calvin, in operating very closely within the biblical historical timeline as expressed within the Judeo-Christian Bible, was strictly against revelations or prophecies that come to the fore outside in the historicity of world history outside the Bible. What the Bible is proclaiming about the Second Coming of Christ—that it is certain he will come again and that we do not know when—is sufficient for Calvin's view.

3.6.2 White's Historicalness of Prophecy Regarding the Second Coming

Brand and McMahon (2005, 29-33), in their book *The Prophet and Her Critics*, deal with some allegations that were made against White's prophecies. The book mentions an allegation that was made by Jonathan Butler in 1979, which accuses White of having "derived her understanding of end-time events" based on the environment that she found herself in and hence that she assumed that the end time was near. Butler collected all the information he could relating to the political and religious mood of her lifetime, and he realized that many were similar to what she had described. He mentioned that White had predicted that spiritualism would be on the rise and that it would be of enormous value in the end time, when actually spiritualism was on the increase by the time she wrote. Hence, Butler concluded that White had actually been predicting the end time of "her world." Purportedly, Butler argued that the events that White had predicted—such as the Sunday laws that would be legislated and the increase of spiritualism, for example—did not gain momentum, but rather went on a decline. Butler alleges, "What Seventh-day Adventists must fully acknowledge here . . . is the element of *prophetic disconfirmation*." By this, Butler meant that White's prophecy was a failed prophecy.

At this juncture, not only am I of the same persuasion as Brand and McMahon, arguing in response to Butler that those events foretold by White will be repeated prior to Christ's Second Coming, I am also of the opinion that Butler has fallen short of being able to see that even if those events were not repeated prior to Christ's Second Coming, White's prophecy would not have been a failed prophecy. We should not be content to merely say, with a repetition of events, that prior to Christ's Second Coming, there will be an increase in spiritualism and Sunday laws will be legislated, etc. Instead, we should allow our minds to stretch to the point of realizing that even if those events are not repeated prior to Christ's Second Coming, White will still not have been wrong in her prediction of what she saw just prior to her death. She will be in perfect harmony with her prediction and Christ's Second Coming, since the only events that she predicted to happen prior to the Second Advent actually transpired before her death. The next moment, for her realization, is Christ's Second Coming. The reason why it is possible that those events might not be repeated is due to the fact that all of God's promises and threats are conditional:

> The angels of God in their messages to men represent time as very short. [See Romans 13:11-12; 1 Corinthians 7:29; 1 Thessalonians 4:15, 17; Hebrews 10:25; James 5:8-9; 1 Peter 4:7; Revelation 22:6-7.] Thus it has always been presented to me. It is true that time has continued longer than we expected in the early days of this message. Our Savior did not appear as soon as we hoped. But has the Word of the Lord failed? Never! It should be remembered

> that the promises and threatenings of God are alike conditional [see Jeremiah 18:7-10; Jonah 3:4-10] . . . We may have to remain here in this world because of insubordination many more years, as did the children of Israel, but for Christ's sake His people should not add sin to sin by charging God with the consequence of their own wrong course of action (White 1992, 39).

Apostles of the early Church predicted the end time to be imminent and that Christ would come during their lifetime. Shall we say that the prophecies of the other apostles as quoted above were false prophets since they prophesied the imminent return of Christ in their day, and almost two thousand years have lapsed and Christ has not come?

> And of His people He said, "Behold . . . I will be their God, in truth and in righteousness." Zechariah 8:3, 7-8 . . . These promises were conditional on obedience. The sins that had characterized the Israelites prior to the captivity were not to be repeated. "Execute true judgment," the Lord exhorted those who were engaged in rebuilding; "and show mercy and compassions every man to his brother: and oppress not the widow, nor the fatherless, the stranger, nor the poor; and let none of you imagine evil against his brother." "Speak ye every man the truth to his neighbor; execute the judgment of truth and peace in your gates" Zechariah 7:9, 10; 8:16 (White [1917] 1943, 704).

White, in her time, was aware of the fact that there were those who had felt that, due to the fact that Jesus did not come, there must have been a failed prophecy. Hence, she wrote:

> The angels of God in their messages to men represent time as very short. Thus it has always been presented to me. It is true that time has continued longer than

> we expected in the early days of this message. Our Savior did not appear as soon as we hoped. But has the word of the Lord failed? Never! It should be remembered that the promises and threatenings of God are alike conditional . . . God had committed to His people a work to be accomplished on earth. The third angel's message was to be given, the minds of believers were to be directed to the heavenly sanctuary, where Christ had entered to make atonement for His people. The Sabbath reform was to be carried forward. The breach in the law of God must be made up. The message must be proclaimed with a loud voice, that all the inhabitants of earth might receive the warning. The people of God must purify their souls through obedience to the truth, and be prepared to stand without fault before Him at His coming (White 1958b, 67).

The point that emerges here is that of the difference in time between a person who dies during the time of the apostle Paul and a person who dies now. When Christ will come and raise the dead, how much different in time will there be for the two parties to the coming of Jesus? When a person dies, time stops. That person is not conscience of the different events that transpire and is not cognizant of the passing on of time. So when both persons awake, the presence of Christ will be sudden, since they will both only recall their existence from the last moment before their death. What may be a seeming delay to those alive, even if one hundred thousand years have transpired, is imminent for those dead, since time is non-existent for them. The Scriptures tell us that the dead have no knowledge or an awareness of the transpiring events on earth (Ecclesiastes 9:5-6).

The point we intend to make here is that Butler's conclusion that White made a failed prophecy is indeed premature, since Christ's Second Coming has not yet taken place. That leaves the window of White's predictions yet possible to unfold.

However, there is the other possibility, which, though it is not the belief of the current writer, should be considered: Butler's argument that White was merely predicting the end time of her own world does not in itself constitute a failed prophecy in that what transpired happened prior to the end of her life time. Christ's coming, therefore, culminates those events. For White, Christ's coming was imminent in that she does not see or experience the passing of time while she lies unconscious in her grave. So when she predicted that Christ is coming, yes, Butler is correct if he is saying that Christ came for her in her time—because she would die in 1915. Jesus will come for her in her time in that when she is resurrected, she will begin to recall the moments of her time before she died. However, Butler is wrong in intimating that her prophecy failed since, White operated analogous with other Bible prophets.

> Now we beseech you, brethren, by the coming of our Lord Jesus Christ, and by our gathering together unto him, That ye be not soon shaken in mind, or be troubled, neither by spirit, nor by word, nor by letter as from us, as that the day of Christ is at hand. Let no man deceive you by any means: for that day shall not come, except there come a falling away first, and that man of sin be revealed, the son of perdition; Who opposeth and exalteth himself above all that is called God, or that is worshipped; so that he as God sitteth in the temple of God, shewing himself that he is God (KJV 1976).

The Classic Bible Commentary, edited by Owen Collins (1999, 1391), says that the words, "is at hand," mean, "is immediately imminent," but literally, "is present" or "instantly coming." Adds Collins:

> It is not likely that Paul would imply anything contrary here; what he denies is that it is so immediately

> imminent, instant, or present, as to justify the neglect of everyday worldly duties.

White, in her time, experienced the same situation as that understood from the Scriptural interpretation of *The Classic Bible Commentary*.

Knight, in his *If I Were The Devil* (2007, 252-253), says that "post-Adventists" had a mixed understanding about the Second Advent of Christ. One group emphasized an immediate coming; the other stressed occupying in transit despite the fact that they all anticipated a no long-delayed day of Christ's Second Coming.

Knight further said that those who held to the former view of immediacy of the Second Advent clung to the sermonizing while most engaged themselves in some form of meaningful work to sustain their family lives. The latter group shunned organized contracts and formal organizational agreements since they deemed such obligations to have implications of some sort of lack of faith in the imminent return of Christ, which would contribute in Christ's delayed advent. Within the rank of those who held to the immediacy of the Second Advent came the allurements of continued date-setting. From this rank were Josiah Litch and William Miller, who anticipated Christ's return to be prior "to the end of the Jewish year 1844," which is spring 1845. Others such as Joseph Marsh and H. H. Gross predicted Christ's day to be 1847. Early Sabbatarian Adventists such as Joseph Bates also set dates. Seven years after the 1844 Disappointment in October 1851, said Bates, Christ would come.

White, on the other hand, was at odds with Bates and the other two founders of the Sabbatarian Adventist movement. Hence, on July 21, 1851, a letter of importance from White was included in the *Review and Herald*:

> Dear Brethren . . . the Lord has shown me that the message of the third angel must go, and be proclaimed to the scattered children of the Lord, and that it

> should not be hung on time; for time never will be a test again. I saw that the third angel's message was stronger than time can be. I saw that this message can stand on its own foundation, and that it needs not time to strengthen it, and that it will go in mighty power, and do its work, and will be cut short in righteousness (*Review and Herald* July 21, 1851).

What is important at this juncture is to understand that White was (as George Knight correctly assessed) opposed to setting a date to Christ's Second Advent because it created "false excitement." Sabbatarians were to realize that their core message is the third angel's message of Revelation 14:9-12 and that that message was stronger than time can be. That message would be coupled with another message for his Remnant Church—Rev. 14:14-20, which for the third angel's message is embedded in verses 9-12. Occupation in daily chores held importance over "eschatological excitement" (Knight 2007, 251-255).

Now this should suffice to help us understand that while White heralded the imminence of Christ's Second Coming, she understood it not to take place so soon that neglect over present daily responsibilities would be shunned. She understood, like the apostle Paul, that the Second Advent would take place after certain events first took place. Hence, we see again that White avoided speculating into date-settings and time with regard to Christ's Second Advent. Instead, White worked with the unique principle of the divine historicity expressed in the historical biblical timeline from which she, in the mirroring of Christ's words, interpreted the words as presenting a clue and a hint regarding signs that will transpire before his Second Advent. She warned against date-setting but underscored what is said, "Verily I say unto you, This generation shall not pass, till all these things be fulfilled . . . But of that day and hour knoweth no man, no, not the angels of heaven, but my Father only" Matthew 24:34; 36 (KJV 1976).

3.7 Summary of Interactional Substantialism

Both White and Calvin are faced with a dilemma and a challenge. Yet as difficult as their challenge is, we see how in the most compelling and awe-inspiring way, they have satisfactorily explicated the tremendous mystery of the divine mysteries of the dual natures of Christ with the limitations of the human language. Commenting on the account of Luke 19:41-44, for instance, we see how White engages the contrasting activities of the two natures of Christ. She says that while Christ was sitting on the colt and making a triumphant entry into Jerusalem, he had intended to show that he was the Lamb of God, Israel's messiah, and king. The contrasts of Christ's two natures are seen in that as a man Christ is depicted as one weeping! As the divine God, he foresees the dark impending doom that awaits Israel as a result of her rejecting her king (who is Jesus). In other words, as a divine being, Christ foresees the impending doom that is to fall upon the undiscerning nation of Israel, who failed to recognize the presence of God through the Son of man Jesus Christ.

Commenting on the same text, Calvin says that Christ's divinity was *resting* (my italics). Calvin is giving opportunity for his [Christ's] humanness to be expressed. This manner of linguistic use is figurative, I believe. Calvin's style in saying that divinity *rested* is that which we read elsewhere in the Bible, which is intended by the narrators to express the inexplicable divine conceptualization experiences, as something relative to the human experience. For example, the Bible says that God rested on the Sabbath day, after creating the world in six days, the animals, the fountains, and all that is in the world and humankind. We are not to interpret the word, "rest," here as though divinity gets tired. The Hebrew word, "rest," in Exodus 20:11 is: וינח *(nû wach)*. It could be translated literally and figuratively as to stay, *to let fall, to dwell, let alone, withdraw, to cease, to be quiet, etc.* (Green 1976, 65; Exodus 19:20).

It could sound almost contradictory to think that a loving, caring God was actually resting in the natural sense of the word *rest*, while the human nature of Christ was suffering emotional pain and grief. However, when we interpret this word to mean that divinity allowed this grief to be expressed through the humanity of Jesus, then it is slightly of different effect for our reciprocity. I believe that Calvin, by his use of the word *rest* in the afore-mentioned context, meant to imply that divinity did not reveal itself in a way that it occasionally did. Even if divinity would have manifested itself, it could always do so in a manner that would express the emotions that are relative to human emotions. White seeks to express these divine emotions through her picturesque language that seeks to portray what the divine nature of Christ must have been experiencing.

> Jesus gazes upon the scene, and the vast multitude hush their shouts, spellbound by the sudden vision of beauty. All eyes turn upon the Savior, expecting to see in his countenance the admiration they themselves feel. But instead of this they behold a cloud of sorrow. They are surprised and disappointed to see his eyes fill with tears, and his body rock to and fro like a tree before the tempest, while a wail of anguish bursts from his quivering lips, as if from the depths of a broken heart. What a sight was this for angels to behold: their loved Commander in an agony of tears! What a sight was this for the glad throng that with shouts of triumph and the waving of palm branches were escorting him to the glorious city, where they fondly hoped he was about to reign! Jesus had wept at the grave of Lazarus, but it was in a godlike grief in sympathy with human woe. But this sudden sorrow was like a note of wailing in a grand triumphal chorus In the midst of a scene of rejoicing, where all were paying Him homage, Israel's King was in tears (White 1940, 575-576).

It is my conviction and opinion that it is this moving, dramatic, and graphic employ of the most vivid figurative language, which White uses to describe the events that ultimately led to the death of Christ on the cross of Golgotha, that was intended to express the mood and the intense indescribable activity within the divine realm. White, like the early writers of the Gospels, describes the violent catastrophe that took place at the scene of Golgotha to evoke the emotions that divinity must have been experiencing. While relating to the events that took place at the cross, Calvin says that the divine nature of Christ was *quiescent*. Commenting on the same events, White says that the Father was with his Son at the cross. She also adds that divinity hid itself in a dark cloud. Certainly, this kind of language should not be taken literally, since God does not need to hide himself in a cloud in order to be invisible.

This is the same way in which Bible writers have described God's emotions, actions, and interactions to certain events of importance. For White to say that God was at the cross with his Son means more than we read at face value. What it means to me is that God manifested himself in a certain way that expresses the grief, pain, shame, and excruciating anguish and trying moment if you will, with regard to the experience and revelation of divinity that is beyond human phanthoming. While the scriptures teach us that nothing is impossible with God, and that nothing is too hard for God, we are not to take flight with the winds of drastically expurgating the spurious notion of a God that is detached from the physical world and is devoid of emotion, pity, life, anger, etc. It does not make sense when we try to understand what White and Calvin are saying if we take their sayings here literally.

God does not need to come down to the cross to be with his Son, since God was always with his Son, and knowing that he is always omnipresent. He does not need to hide himself in a cloud since he is invisible to the human eye anyway. The same is true with the notion of God having turned his back on his Son. God does not need to turn around in order to get around. Christ's divinity does not need to rest, since divinity does not require rest at any point, bearing in mind that God does not need to repose into a state of idleness. Therefore, Calvin's and White's words should not always be literally interpreted, but they should be interpreted in context in order to understand their intended meaning.

What should suffice is that both White and Calvin have employed language that they best knew in order to attempt to explicate to mortals that which is eminently, enormously, beyond the facets and realms of human fathoming. However, it is equally a truce to acknowledge that divinity, in its infinite distance and vastness, which supersedes humanity's ability to conceptualize its true nature, there is still evidence beyond doubt that human logic is able to comprehend, in relative terms, the emotions and activities of God that he allows us to know.

If we are to envisage that premise of a literal interpretation and understanding of the Father as having turned his back on the sight of his Son, whose visage had been one of a heap of all the sins of the world, then we could also allow ourselves to perceive a transitory moratorium of *the Trinitarian* partnership of which Christ continued to be a sharer thereof while he was on earth, since his inception at the incarnation. What I seek to deduce here is that there is never a time that God in unison ever separated in the real sense. Divinity has deemed it fit that we would understand, know, participate, and experience God in and through Jesus Christ.

This linguist picturesque is the human instrument's utmost attempt to convey to mortals the immense intensity and interactions within the realm of divinity. In her vision, White purports to have been privileged to be captivated in vision. She relates how she saw Christ in that vision, before he came to earth as a man, pleading with his Father that he may become the ransom for fallen humanity. Describing in graphic terms, White states:

> Three times He [Christ] was shut in by the glorious light about the Father, and the third time He came from the Father, His person could be seen. His countenance was calm, free from all perplexity . . . said the angel, "Think ye that the Father yielded up His dearly beloved Son without a struggle?" No, no. It was even a struggle with the God of heaven, whether to let guilty man perish, or to give His beloved Son to die for him (White [1882] 1945a, 149-151).

Looking at this scene and interpreting the words employed by White, we may declare that there was hesitation, doubt, and reluctance from the Father before allowing his Son to be a bearer of sinful humanity's lot. However, bearing in mind that the plan of salvation was devised by God in unison, in the midst of eternity's past, before the foundations of the world, makes it most unlikely that there could be shock, doubt, or hesitation on the part of God in implementing what had been agreed upon within the Godhead and remained a mystery and a secret that was hid and kept in silence by God (Romans 16:25). Nevertheless, I believe this personification of God, as depicted by White, is an inference on the ignominy and complexity on the part of divinity revealed to humanity. What inspiration intended for us through these writings is that mankind should behold and reciprocate the immeasurable gift of God—God giving himself to estranged humanity. The language employed is intended to communicate the incomprehensible, matchless, and priceless gift of God to his erring wayward children. Hence, interpretation is again essential when we read what White writes.

Having said this, I do not mean to suggest that White's account of what she declares to have seen is not a literal one. Instead, I uphold that the literal account must be interpreted in as much as the Bible narrations ought to be interpreted, since spiritual things ought to be spiritually discerned. We are encouraged by Saint Paul to study the Scriptures: "Study to show yourself approved unto God, a workman that needeth not to be ashamed, rightly dividing the word of truth" (2 Timothy 2:15, KJV 1976).

3.8 Monolithic Mono- and Dual-Substantialist View of Decoding Jesus

3.8.1 First Millennium Mono- and Dual-Substantialist Views

The history of the well-known deviations and so-called heresies of the first millennium is cursorily dealt with in order to get to a better understanding of mono- and dual-substantialist views of the first millennium. These views could at the same time function as background to modern liberal mono-substantialist and modern interactional-substantialist views, such as those of White and Calvin.

3.8.1.1 Arianism

First, we shall look at the doctrine of Arius. Arianism arose as a heresy from Alexandria, which was condemned at the first General Council of Nicea in 325. According to Arius, God was the only one, beside whom there is no other and who is pure in simplicity and spirituality. God, as the only one, created of his free will before the world existed, an independent substance—the Son of God—as the instrument by means of which all other creatures were to be created. The Son is not a creature like other creatures, but is a special creature, who, in the process of God's bestowal of grace and by his own gradual moral progress, has become God so that we now call him "only begotten God," "strong God," and so on (Harnack 1961, 15-19).

This means in the follow-up process of the incarnation and the human side of the Son of God that the Arians could not accept the notion of immediate incarnation, in which the divinity and the humanity were fused into one with the emphasis on the divine side. Thus, God does not become man, but rather they opted for the position in which the Son of God, Christ, the *Logos*—with no human soul—being capable of suffering, not an absolute perfect being, but one who by truly taking on and adopting a human body by effort attains absolute perfection. Christ is thus not an absolute perfect being, but through the process of progress in the adopted state of the human body, and by being attached to human feelings, attains by effort absolute perfection (19). The Arians with their view of *homoiousios*—Christ is like God—lost out to the Athanasians, who fully drew the strongest conclusions from the notion of *homoousios*, which was Christ is God (49).

3.8.1.2 Pneumatomachianism

The Pneumatomachians were semi-Arians who purposely developed the doctrine of the Holy Spirit in the fourth century in opposition to the notion of *homoousia*—Christ is God (Harnack 1961, 114). Macedonius (d. 354), the highly esteemed leader of the Thracian semi-Arians and at a later stage the deposed bishop of Constantinople, defended the doctrine that the Spirit is a creature similar to the angels, a being subordinate to the Father and the Son and in their service. To Macedonius, the Holy Scripture does not describe the Holy Spirit as an object of adoration, and he pointed out that the relation of Father and Son did not admit of a third partner (Harnack 1961, 114). The second General Council of Constantinople condemned him in 381CE.

Pneumatomachianism claimed to acknowledge the divinity of Christ, and yet they denied the deity of the Holy Ghost. What is at stake here is that while the *homoiousians* usually operated with the view that "Christ is like God," which became "Christ is God," they shifted their *homoiousian* view to the Holy Spirit. Thus, the Holy Spirit is a creature, similar to the angels, like God but is not God-self but a divine energy. The Pneumatomachians, or semi-Arians, while starting to acknowledge that in the incarnation the Son is equal to the Father, still deny the Holy Spirit to be fully God.

3.8.1.3 Apollonarianism

The Council of Constantinople (381) dealt with the heresy of Apollonarianism, which derived its name from the churchman and theologian Apollinaris. At first, Apollinaris was held in high regard by his contemporaries. According to Harnack:

> Epiphanius treated Apollinaris in a friendly fashion, Athanasius corresponded with him, the Cappadocians at first revered him and always held him in high respect, while the Arian theologians extolled him as their ablest opponent (Harnack 1961, 49).

Apollonaris (d. 392), who was the bishop of Laodicea, at first in combating Arianism with its changeable Christ, started by allowing that the assumption that in Christ, God as *Logos*, who is equal to Christ in substance, united himself with a physically perfect man out of necessity, which led to the idea of two Sons of God: one natural and one adopted. Thus, according to Apollinaris, two knowing and two willing beings could not possibly be united in one being. According to Harnack, there are three theses that Apollinaris attacks and from which one can easily understand what his own theology was:

> He wishes to disown (1) the view that there are two sons, (2) the idea that Christ was an *άν θρ ώπ ος έν θε ος* [human being in God], the view he attributed to Marcellus, since heathens and Jews could also believe in a Christ of this kind, (3) the view that Christ is a free and therefore a changeable being (Harnack 1961, 151).

In accordance with these dissertations, he directed his attacks first against the gnostic tendency among various contemporaries in which a strong division is made between Christ and Jesus; second, against Paul of Samosata, Marcellus, and Photinus; and finally, against Origen and Arius. Apollinaris' approach boils down to the following: Christ was not merely an inspired man, but must have assumed our nature in such a way that he made it the perfect organ of his Godhead. As it was with many of his contemporaries and predecessors, the prototypical biblical statement of "the Word (*logos*) became flesh (*sarx*)" was understood in terms of his sense-making approach. We have seen that this statement meant within Arius' views that the Word or *Logos* adopted or assumed a human being, while in many of the other incarnational views doing the rounds, the Word or *Logos* had a predisposed inclination in pre-existence to become flesh. In Apollinaris' view, the statement that the Word became flesh meant that Christ was found as a man (Harnack 1961, 152). Apolinaris works on the basis that Christ appeared both in the likeness of sinful flesh and in the likeness of men. On one hand, in him there was the most perfect unity of the human and the divine so that what could be said about the humanity holds true for the divinity and vice versa—for instance, that God was born and dies, and so on. On the other hand, the Godhead, in Apollinaris' view, is not to be thought of as capable of suffering. The flesh, the human nature, is divine. Apollinaris states:

> The flesh therefore is divine, because it is united with God, and it indeed saves (quoted in Harnack 1961, 153).

The *Logos*, the Word, certainly did not bring his flesh with him from heaven, but he is nevertheless the "heavenly man" because it was intended that in the essence of the *Logos*, he was the mediator between God and humanity. Thus, in the historical incarnation, everything in this heavenly man should be divine. Death could be overcome only if it was God who suffered and died. The human side is purely the passive element only, the organ of the Godhead and the object of reconciliation and redemption (Harnack 1961, 154).

3.8.1.4 Nestorianism

In the Nestorian controversy, around (428-433 A.D.), the view of incarnation comprises the necessity to maintain that God as *Logos* assumed a perfect man from the race of David and united such a man with himself. God as *Logos* was dwelling in the man Jesus from the time of the conception. This indwelling is made sense of in a similar way as the general indwelling of God in human beings. The central notion of the Nestorians amounts to dwelling in or indwelling that is not a substantial indwelling, which would mean a transmutation of the humanity of Christ, or on the other hand, a limiting of the Godhead (Harnack 1961, 167). Nor is it any mere indwelling of inspiration. It is a gracious indwelling in which God out of grace, and in accordance with his own good pleasure, has united himself with the man Jesus in the way he unites himself with every pious soul. The only difference is that in the case of Jesus, the union was, besides being perfect, also in virtue of the gradual moral growth to perfection through his piety. The indwelling is to be seen as a kind of combination (ςυ *νά θε ιά*), or it may be expressed in the following mixed metaphorical way: God dwells in the man as in a temple (Harnack 1961, 167). Nestorius (d. 451) rejected the notion that Mary was the *Theotokos* (i.e., God-bearer). By so doing, he implied that the person of the Son and the person of Christ were two diverse persons who were unified by a nominal kind of relationship.

Nestorianism, which was condemned at the third council at Ephesus in 431, arose out of Constantinople. It was more specifically condemned at the fifth general council at Constantinople in 533. The union between the divinity and the humanity of Christ was relative, and since each nature in Christ is at the same time person, it was here that the peculiar difficulty arises. The union was in the last resort only nominal, and they had two persons in Christ: a divine and a human one (Harnack 1961, 168). Nestorianism had been regarded as a heresy because its indwelling view of incarnation brought about a very loose connection between the divinity and humanity of Christ.

3.8.1.5 Monophysitism

The pendulum moved from the Nestorian dualistic view of Christ to a mono-substantialist controversy, called Monophysitism and Eutychianism, around 448-451 A.D. Monophysitism supported the view of transforming Jesus the human being into an eternal being, and Eutychianism tended more in the direction of a "blending" and "confusion" of the two natures with the emphasis clearly on the divine side (Harnack 1961, 200). Differences between the mono-substantialists at the time were minimal; however, they saw a difference between the formulas such as "one incarnate nature of the *Logos*" and "one nature of the incarnate *Logos*" (Harnack 1961, 236). The mono-substantialists taught that Jesus' humanity was absorbed into his divinity so that his humanity no longer existed as created humanity. Though the champion of Monophysitism, Severus, defended himself against the supposition that he taught that the human nature of Christ loses its natural peculiarity in the union with the divinity, and was thus transformed into something eternal, the total sense-making approach boils down to Christ's humanity as being transformed into something eternal (Harnack 1961, 239-241). According to Harnack:

> Here already we meet with the thought that something created can nevertheless be something eternal. We hear no more of a flesh, which was brought hither from heaven, but a kindred idea takes the place of this heretical thought (1961, 240).

This brand of mono-substantialism emerged out of Constantinople and received its condemnation by the fourth General Council in 451 at Chalcedon.

3.8.1.6 Monothelitism

The Monothelitism controversy—about 630-680 A.D.—emerged, on one hand, between proponents who advocated the doctrine of the one will in reference to Jesus Christ, in the sense that his human nature was wholly filled with the divine will or his divinity (God-*Logos*) was regarded as the subject of the God-Man Jesus Christ. And on the other hand, Pope Leo put a viewpoint forward in a doctrinal letter that each nature does what is peculiar to it in union with the other. Such a formulation was new to the eastern part of the Church, and the various mono-substantialist proponents in the east moved in the direction that Christ has two energies and two wills (Harnack 1961, 252-253). Monothelitism taught that Jesus Christ had one will, but two natures. The Orthodox position is contrary to this position since it teaches that Jesus possessed two natures and two wills, the human and divine wills. Monothelitism is a product that developed from the Monophysite position through the Christological debates. During the seventh century, Monothelitism enjoyed a great deal of support before it was aborted as a heretical doctrine.

The Chalcedon Christological definition of 451 A.D. spelled out that Christ Jesus was a composite of two natures in one person, without referring to the notion of energies and wills. Chalcedon was in clear opposition to the extreme Monophysite position, which taught that Jesus was one person consisting of one nature, and the Monotheletic position, which advocated the idea that in Jesus one divine energy and one divine will operated. In the whole era during which the controversy stretched, accusations were made that from today's perspective are no longer valid.

Nestorius, for instance, was accused of teaching the doctrine of two wills, while a reading of the work, *Ekthesis pistews*, of Heraclius of 638 clearly shows that it was not the case. Emperor Heraklius in 633 suggested through the Patriarch of Constantinople, Sergius I (610-638), a wonderful compromise stating that everything in Christ that exists out of two natures operates through a God-man driven energy or activity (*mia Theandrike energeia*). After Heraclius published his works, Pope Honorius made a dogma in an effort to forbid any mention of one or two energies, one or two wills. In this dogma, he stated that Christ had, in himself, only a single will (*en Thelema*), thereby letting monothelitism—the "one-will-approach"—win the day (Walker 1985, 182).

3.8.2 Modern Liberal Monolithic Substantialism

3.8.2.1 Introduction

In this section, a general description is presented of the broad sense-making approach of the modern era, in which the two-nature approach toward Christ has been turned around and transformed into a monolithic substantialist approach, which only encapsulates the humanity of Jesus and fixes the reflexive schemes on his true humanity. Any talk of his divinity is fitted into the human being Jesus' experience of God. The question one has to ask in this regard is how liberal humanists could make sense of Jesus Christ as a mortal human being who is capacitated with extraordinary skills, enabling him to change and transform people to live a better life.

3.8.2.2 Some Trajectories of Monolithic Substantialism

What we really seek to examine here is the modern liberal humanist concept of how and where Jesus Christ's life, death, and resurrection fit into the grand acts of God's creation; God's reconciliation circumscribed in the life, death, and resurrection of Jesus Christ; God's renewal through Pentecost; and God's consummation and fulfillment of all things culminating in the new heaven and the new earth.

There is a vast difference between the sense-making worlds of Calvin and White and the liberal human-centered approach of the Bible. Calvin and White operated with the notion of the Bible in which the biblical historical timeline expresses God's revelational history with human beings and the natural cosmic world, set within the array of God's grand acts of creation, reconciliation, renewal, and fulfillment, and the liberal human-centered view of the Bible plainly views the Bible as a composition of written documents deriving from oral traditions and eyewitness experience of people about God, human beings, and the natural world.

In the liberal humanist approach, some parts of the Bible refer to actual history and other parts to a mythical depiction of certain events. In this regard, liberal humanists are accused of not necessarily believing in the actual realness and accuracy of the biblical record, while opponents admit they view certain elements of the biblical history from a perspective of realness and actuality. Largely, they view the events around Christ's crucifixion and his associates as real characters of the Bible who are believed to have existed in certain earthly locations.

The main question is how does such a type of liberal humanist, sense-making, God-human-nature approach operate in the downgrading of the Bible to a collection of books only depicting the experience of human beings about God, themselves, other human beings, and the natural cosmic world? The question of importance here is what is a downgraded Jesus Christ, as an exclusively unique and extraordinary human being, supposed to look like? Any talk of his divinity is relegated to the level of the presence of God in this unique and particular human being's life and experience.

Two main trajectories in the current world are, to a large extent, expressive of the liberal humanistic view of the identity of Christ. The first trajectory is that of gnostic and mystic views of Jesus. The second trajectory is the multiple science fiction renditions of Jesus, which are contributions to the liberal humanistic ideology of the conception of Jesus' identity as that of a mere mortal constructed through the efforts of scientific humanist scholarship.

In both these trajectories, Jesus is viewed as an enlightened mere mortal human being with extraordinary spiritual powers. Both these trajectories in their modern versions have been influenced by the older humanist tradition, going back to the era of ancient Greece and the humanist views in the early Roman Empire, which influenced humanism of the Renaissance (1350-1550) and the Reformation of the sixteenth century. The humanist approaches about Jesus in the Reformation influenced the humanist approaches of the eighteenth-century Enlightenment, and the hundreds of nineteenth century studies in which the life of Jesus was investigated from the standpoint of liberal human consciousness. The Jesus found and constructed in each of the investigations was a replica of the consciousness of the investigator. With these historical periods as background, we only refer to modern gnostic and mystic approaches to Jesus and the modern science fiction approach to Jesus.

3.8.2.3 Christ's Monolithic Nature

In this section, we are mainly referring to two mono-substantialist views of our modern era. One is the modern gnostic and mystic approach, and the other is the science fiction approach of people like Dan Brown. It is interesting that the modern humanist approaches are contra-views to the traditional historical monotheliticism, which taught that Jesus was a composite of two natures, whereas liberal humanism claims that Jesus consists of one human nature. In this view, Jesus is just a mid-eastern Jewish man and nothing else.

The first mono-substantialist view has to do with the many current gnostic and mystic humanist approaches that hark back to ancient gnostic and mystic histories within and outside Christianity. Various church fathers described the gnostics as a perversion of what Christendom is. However, almost all scholars today disagree with the view of the church fathers, due to the available evidence. There is no academic concord with regard to the origins of gnosticism and mysticism and the multiple sense-making approaches that operated as undercarriages for the different views.

According to some, Judaism is somewhat, in one way or another, linked to gnosticism. Some believe that the Old Testament texts demonstrate many gnostic features, and others view the Gospels of the New Testament, and especially the writings and letters of Paul, as permeated with gnostic references. Gnostic elements are also found in the writings of the ancient Greek philosophers such as Aristotle and Plato. In the discovery of the Nag Hammadi texts, there was a partial find of the philosopher Plato's work, entitled the *Republic*. While it appears to some that gnosticism may have roots in Iranian religious practices or some eastern religions that may have stemmed from Zoroastrianism, that inference remains inconclusive. What is certain though is that the many gnostic and mystic approaches in the past were very "syncretistic," gathering and sifting enlightenment clues and sparks from nearly every viewpoint that suits the purpose of the enlightened adherents. In this sense, the adherents of gnostic and mystic movements employed diverse religious ideologies to enhance their intended course of mission (Douglas [1962] 1986, 426).

Regarding current gnosticism and mysticism as an expression of the one human nature approach, Jesus is viewed as "the" human being who had and still has "a divine spark," which descended from "the divine realm above," and which, in terms of continuous growth, makes all of us participants of the spiritual cosmos. The following provides a description of the movement of the divine spark in gnostic approaches:

> Gnostic sects were of the belief that the individual human had "a divine spark" in him/her which descended from "the divine realm above" and fell into this planet in which there is death, birth and fate. According to this notion, this spark can be aroused or woken up by its "divine counterpart" and may

> be reintroduced as a participant into the spiritual cosmos (*Encyclopaedia Britannica* 1982c, 214).

Modern gnostic and mystic approaches about Jesus and people's salvific and spiritual growth patterns see it as part of spiritual growth to gather divine sparks, not only from the Bible but simultaneously from one's involvement with different interpretations and other text applications, such as the alternate Gospels of the Nag Hammadi library and many of the gnostic Gospels regarding Jesus' teachings. Their main problem with traditional Christianity is that the deeper gnostic and mystic spirituality of Paul's writings and the biblical Gospels are not recognized and acknowledged. Yet fundamentalist-mirroring Christians, viewing the Bible as inerrant and infallible, ridicule gnostic and mystic myths and narratives, which in many respects are similar to some of the central doctrines of their fundamentalist mindset (Ostow 1990, 105f).

Modern gnostics and mystics, however, regard the myth of the "inerrant and infallible" text of the Bible, emerging in the modern era, of every little letter and verse divinely endorsed and authorized, as the main stumbling block in the quest for a deeper spiritual meaning of Jesus (Ostow 1990, 101). The second regressive step, according to modern gnostics and mystics, is undertaken by claiming that these inerrant and infallible divine texts express real history that supposedly has to function as the main template of application of all world history outside the divine text. According to these modern gnostics and mystics, traditional Christians who work with the divine revelational historical timeline affix their divine schemes to the surface of the texts, and had therefore very little understanding of the esoteric symbolic meanings that the gnostics and mystics viewed as written into the deeper layers of the biblical texts.

The modern gnostic and mystic viewpoint and the liberal humanist's point of mono-substantialism regarding the man Jesus are not difficult to link. The liberal humanist position envisaged in Jesus a man with an extraordinary talent, but a mere man with spiritual powers demonstrating a spiritual growth pattern that nearly no other human being has acquired. According to this approach, Jesus was able to do mighty works through his spiritual enlightenment, and he was able to move many people, including us, who could be enabled spiritually of doing similar mighty works. Gnostic and mystic approaches of the past and the present derived their strength from their belief in the power that permeates the depths of being human. This belief in the deep underlying powers of human beings provided the insights and enabled a liberal humanistic thinker like Brown to write in a style called science fiction, which sent shockwaves throughout our world.

The second mono-substantialist view has to do with the science fiction approach of people like Dan Brown and is aligned with the modern gnostic and mystic approaches of Jesus.

James L. Garlow, in his book, *The Da Vinci Code Breaker* (2006, 12), makes reference to Peter Jones, who pointed out that:

> God, to Dan Brown, is not the transcendent, above-and-beyond God portrayed in the Bible. God is creation itself—something within me. It (god) is, in fact, me. I don't look to the Bible for truth. I simply look within.

However, Garlow argues that most gnostics were Docetists, who viewed Jesus' appearance as human but regarded him as not truly human. Therefore, I concur with Garlow that there is a conflict of belief between Brown and the gnostics, whom Brown claims, are his sources. Brown perceived Jesus to be a mortal man, while Docetists, of whom many gnostics were, saw Jesus to be a divine something with the appearance of a human being (Garlow 2006, 71).

This old gnostic idea of "self-enlightenment" survived its way through the Renaissance to the eighteenth-century Enlightenment into the works of many German philosophers, who had a commonly viewed design of the sun as the central enlightening agency that shines in a similar sense as enlightened human reason brightly through the parting clouds of the darkness of human bondage. The caption of human reason and rationality as "light dispelling darkness" was often inscribed in many philosophical works in order to ensure that the message was not missed. The self-awareness of philosophers of the Enlightenment was that someone who makes use of his or her own powers and strengths has arrived as a human being devoid of fear. The main premise of this Enlightenment period was that the sun enlightens and frees people from darkness, and human reason enlightens and presents people with the courage to be aware of their own strengths and powers as human beings. All in all, enlightenment, in the eighteenth century sense of the word, was an attempt to shed light upon a world that was plagued with faiths of ignorance, oppressive priests, repressive governments, and opinions that were void of scientific proof.

In his work, *Humanism*, Vernon cites the following:

> The leitmotif of the Enlightenment had probably originated elsewhere. In England, historians have pushed its inception all the way back to the Glorious Revolution of 1688 when many of the issues that became non-negotiable to Enlightenment thinkers, and subsequently contemporary humanism, were written into English law: freedom of the individual, habeas corpus, religious toleration, parliamentary rule and, of course, the rule of law itself. There was a marked intellectual flourishing in England at this time, too, that found a variety of expressions in the publication of pamphlets and newspapers, the opening of public libraries and a widespread interest

> in the theater. These developments were heralded as symptomatic of an enlightened age (2008, 55).

In 1704, the genius, Isaac Newton (1642-1727), whose famous book, *Principia Mathematica*, on the principles of mathematics, progressed to overthrow Aristotle's science by introducing the fundamentals of the laws of motion and gravity. He defined gravity to be time action at a distance. Newton, with the philosopher Leibniz, was regarded as discovering the whole idea of mathematical calculus. The Enlightenment swept through Scotland and was made evident by great greats such as the economist Adam Smith (1723-90) and Adam Ferguson (1723-1816). Among the philosophers were Thomas Reid (1710-90) and David Hume (1711-76). In France, a new birth of Enlightenment manifested itself in the well-known Voltaire.

Since the seventeenth century, French philosophers had been inventing and developing themes for the Enlightenment. Some of these themes evoked questions concerning the connection and difference of God, human beings, and the natural cosmic environment, which were in the majority of instances decided in favor of the innate strengths and powers of human beings and the intrinsic powers of the natural cosmic environment. Religious tolerance was fostered, and the existence of God was investigated through scientific methods. Increasingly, the powers and strengths of God fell at the wayside of scientific and philosophical discussions. The increasing self-awareness of the strengths and powers of human beings not only undergirded the scientific understanding of modern political and social bodies, but also has been the driving impetus in the establishment of democracy and the increasing role of capitalism in the world. In a similar sense, the belief in these strengths and powers provided the rationale for the struggle between human morality deriving from human rationality and divine faith (Vernon 2008, 56).

At this point, Dan Brown's approach of science fiction is important; it amounts to an approach of a mixing of a so-called scientific mentality with "scientifically constructed facts" about Jesus that fit the molds of his scientific method.

Both the approaches of the modern gnostics and mystics and Dan Brown's science fiction approach are very divergent from the positions of Calvin and White, who did not perceive Christ to be encapsulated solely in his humanity and thus be exactly like every one of us. Their view amounts to that Christ is exactly like every one of us as human beings, but totally not like us at the same time as God in the highest possible sense.

3.8.2.4 Christ Identity, Role, and Function in a Monolithic Substantialist Approach

Here, the question is whether Christ's life has or had meaning for anyone else than himself. In other words, did Christ have any salvific meaning for other people? How the salvific significance of Jesus is viewed in gnosticism can be of help to us. One has to take note that in gnosticism, Jesus is not an indispensable necessity to the quest of humankind's salvation.

The terms gnosis, gnostic, and gnostics in their current usage are loaded, depending from which sense making approach these terms are tackled. Speaking in general terms, one can say that the notion of gnosis (or gnosticism), describes a type of knowledge that follows an inner moral and spiritual growth path of increasing self-awareness and self-realization with the underlying belief that there is an "entity or causal factor" called God and of whom people's real awareness and realization of the human self are derivative notions.

Gnostic spiritual growth is essentially "work in progress" into the inner self. Thus, spiritual wisdom in the making is growing day by day. Basic to gnostic philosophy is the recognition, therefore, that gnosis can only be personal and all that people can do for one another is to help by listening and prompting each other to pursue truth and personal realization in a caring way. Gnostics in the sense of day-by-day growth and self-realization do not recognize "universal unchanging doctrines" as taking care of their spiritual needs. To the gnostics, Jesus was to be followed in one's own unique way. Having "faith" in Jesus meant to be belief in him as experiential example of what he taught through his life and to be "faithful" to his ideas is to aspire to become like him, a unique truthful spiritual hero.

Gnosis yields redemption, and Elaine Pagels says that Irenaeus tells us that for the Valentinians gnosis was the redemption of the inner, spiritual man and not the body or the soul. She explains that gnosis could be sensitively translated as "insight." God has to be looked for inside oneself rather than externally (1989, xix). According to the Gospel of Thomas (saying three), Jesus said:

> If you look for the kingdom of God in heaven or in the sea, the birds and the fish will precede you. Rather, the kingdom is inside you, and it is outside you. When you come to know yourselves, then you will become known, and you will realize that it is you who are the sons of the Father. But if you will not know yourselves, you dwell in poverty and it is you who are in poverty (Pagels 1989, xix).

In the early days of the Christian era, the gnostic groups were more attractive to non-Jewish Christians as a new but more realistic religious approach amongst the mystery religions. These groupings continued to exist openly for many centuries until suppressed by the official church establishment. Many church fathers complained about the gnostic elements in their churches. The church fathers objected that these gnostic groupings agreed in general terms with the creeds, and they held informal and unauthorized private meetings to practice their private "heretic beliefs" after church meetings (Riley 1997, 147).

In the gospels of the New Testament, Pagels says (1994, 3):

> The claim is made that Jesus rose once from the dead, bodily, and disappeared bodily into heaven. The Gospel of Philip is another gnostic gospel, found at Nag Hammadi, and it ridicules this idea as the faith of fools. It says the Resurrection is a moment of transformation of existence. The Resurrection is moving from death to spiritual life. It is very much like some Buddhist teachings, talking about moving toward the moment of enlightenment and the understanding of reality. They do not deny the possibility or even the reality of life after death. What they don't believe in is bodily life after bodily death.

It is interesting that the early Church, even in the times of Clement and Origen in Alexandria, still had an approach of double-bookkeeping, distinguishing between the gnostic section as representing the more mature Christians in relation to the other "believers." Pagels says:

> At Alexandria, Origen sometimes argued that all four gospels were partly historical and partly symbolical while relating the first mainly to the first phase of spiritual development and the latter esoteric interpretation to a more mature spirituality. Gnosticism is not so much being born again or instantaneous enlightenment (that may come later), but a willingness to make some sort of spiritual search. At least that is what the Gospel of Thomas says (Pagels 1994, 4).

Pagels comments that what is different about the gnostic Gospels is that they have different perceptions of Jesus. The Gospel of John says he is the only begotten Son of God, and if you believe in him, you are saved. If you don't believe in him, you are condemned. The Gospel of Thomas says, "If you come to know yourselves, then you will know that it is you who are the children of God, and the kingdom of God will be found within." Therefore, "the message here is that every person can discover that he is, so to speak, Jesus' twin brother" (Pagels 1994, 4).

Experiential and intuitive insight that comes from a contemplative life is the name of the gnostic game. Any higher spiritual knowledge of God comes from the Spirit of God within people, and this category of "higher wisdom" mainly derives from intuition as seeing into the inner self. Personal inner intuitive or insightful experience into the inner self portrays itself in a form of "gnosis" as the right kind of spiritual knowledge. People who subscribe to such special, experiential or intuitive, non-ordinary-scientific knowledge are "gnostics." We cannot verify "gnosis" scientifically or objectify gnostic knowledge in a scientific factual way as was the case with hard core science or even in a scientific fictional way as is the case with Dan Brown's soft-swing attempt at a blend of science and fiction.

The idea of Jesus being a messiah and the mediator between humanity and divinity, as portrayed by Calvin and White, is rejected by ancient gnostic, modern gnostic, and mystic views, as well as in the science fiction approach of Brown. The approach of modern-day New Agers is one of the many gnostic and mystic approaches that believes that every one of us may experience God in our personal individual manner (Lutzer 2005, 17).

So the question still lingers: Does the liberalistic humanistic movement perceive Christ's identity as that of a prophet or of a messiah, who would be of salvific-significance to God's helpless people, who are in dire need of divine salvation? Noteworthy in this context is that the majority of ancient gnostic and mystic schools were fundamentally against the idea that God become flesh in the material sense of the word. According to the ancient gnostic points of departure, the material or matter side of creation has to be considered either as evil or at least as worthlessly neutral when compared to spiritual growth. They reasoned that since human beings have matter as one of its components, conjoined with a divine part, human beings were evil or worthless at least.

The salvific view of the gnostics amounts to self-salvation and self-enlightenment in a similar sense as Buddhist approaches. Gnostics also taught that their constructed deity was androgynous with the dual-encompassing qualities of masculine and feminine attributes. Furthermore, gnostics renounced the real bodily resurrection of Jesus, and some of the gnostics even denied that Jesus actually died on the cross. Instead, some even taught that someone else was substituted in the death of Christ—that is, died in his stead. Although there was a dysfunctional harmony with regard to how salvation was received, there was a symphonic concord that redemption rests within the power and strength of every personal individual human being. The greatest need, according to ancient and modern gnostic schemes, is not a need to be saved from *sin* but a *need for self-knowledge, self-awareness, self-realization, and self-actualization.* This redemption is achievable through a direct personal encounter with God, the great mystery of mysteries without the Church or the mediation of Christ (Lutzer 2005, 23-24).

3.9 Transformational Substantialism

The approach of transformational substantialism is closely linked to the history of the Roman Catholic Church. Transubstantiation is the transformation process by which an ordinary human being or natural entity acquires the status of a holy, sacralized, and sacramentalized divine being or entity. There are various transformed sacralized and sacramentalized forms to be found within the holy sacramental and sacred space of the Church. The holy form of all forms is the holy template Jesus, the human being, transformed through the virgin birth of the blessed Mary into a holy, sacred, and sacramental sacrificial divine offer, Christ. The transforming process, taking place in the holy, sacred, and sacramental template Jesus Christ—accompanied by the blessed mother Mary—is over and over enacted, employed, applied, and offered in every corner and pinnacle of the holy sacramental and sacred space of the Church. The total sacralized hierarchical structure of the holy office and office bearers, pope and priests, and the sacred and sacramental offerings of the Seven Sacraments are expressive of the transformational template Jesus, as human being, continuously being transformed into the sacrificial divine offer, Christ.

In a similar sense, as it is with many churches, the central approach that rules the waves in the Roman Catholic Church is embodied in the day-to-day forms, rituals, habits, and prescripts of the Church, and is expressive of the "practical theology" of the congregational and diocesan experience. This sort of practical theology in the everyday sense of the word has come a long way through many centuries, and in spite of minor changes in different global contexts, stayed generally true to the Roman Catholic ethos. The notion of transformational transubstantiation, for instance, made its presence felt during acrimonious twelfth-century debates over the Eucharist. The main line of argument in the debates revolved around the type of transformation process that the elements of ordinary bread and wine actually underwent in the Eucharist. The elements changed into a sacred and sacramental type in which the elements were transformed into the actual body and blood of Jesus Christ, despite their physical appearance to the naked eye.

A ruling was enacted during the Fourth Lateran Council in 1215 that Christ's body and blood were actually captivated and contained in the physical bread and wine, meaning that the power of the Lord Almighty transubstantiated the bread into the body of Christ and the wine into his blood. It was Thomas Aquinas (1225-1274) who affirmed that once the consecration had been made, the actual bread and wine dissipated and the proper conversion took place, which is called transubstantiation (Gonzales 1984: 272,

347-349). The main carrier concept of transformational substantialism (that is, transubstantiation) had been firmly established in the Roman Catholic Church by the middle of the fifteenth century, was declared official doctrine by the Council of Constance (1414-18 A.D.), and confirmed as official doctrine in response to the critique of the Protestant Reformation during the Council of Trent (1545-1563). The Council of Trent in its thirteenth session on the notion of transubstantiation (October 11, 1551) declared:

> And because that Christ, our Redeemer, declared that which He offered under the species of bread to be truly His own body, therefore has it ever been a firm belief in the Church of God, and this holy Synod doth now declare it anew, that, by the consecration of the bread and the wine, a conversion is made of the whole substance of the bread into the substance of the body of Christ our Lord, and of the whole substance of the wine into the substance of His blood; which conversion is, by the holy Catholic Church, suitably and properly called Transubstantiation (Waterworth 1848, 78).

Transubstantiation in the Mass means that through the uttering of the words by which the sacrament had been instituted ("this is my body," etc.) the bread turns physically into the body of Christ, and wine turns physically into the blood of Christ. This miraculous act can only be done by somebody who is authorized to do it—that is, the priest. The act of citing the words of institution as such brings about the change. It means out of the operation flows the change (*ex opera operato*). This act is called consecration. Roughly speaking, the doctrine expects that we believe in two changes—from the natural to the supernatural, from the ordinary to the holy, sacramental and sacred state. First, the bread is now "body" and the wine is "blood." Second, the "body" and the "blood" still look like bread and wine. Thus, in terms of transformational substantialist language, it means that the substance or essence changes while the observable features of bread and wine stays the same.

At a certain point in the liturgical procedure, a bell is rung to mark the precise time of the transformation of the substances into the body and blood of Christ. From this point on, the elements must be handled with care. Because of the danger that some of the "blood" may be spilled, lay members are given only the bread, not the wine. It was assumed that the blood was contained in the body, so those who only received the body missed very little. The "host" (the consecrated bread) is stored away safely in a little cupboard near the altar. It can be carried to the sick and used there without being newly consecrated. When believers enter the church or pass the altar, they bow down deeply because their Lord is physically present there. The host is also sometimes carried through the streets in processions to present the presence of Christ to the public. This is done on a special day called the day of the Body of Christ (*Corpus Christi*).

Though the doctrine of transubstantiation usually revolved around the Eucharist, regarding the elements of bread and wine on one hand and the body and blood of Christ on the other, the whole procedure of transformational substantialization has found its finest expression in the holy, sacred, and sacramental template Jesus Christ. The archetypical and prototypical paradigm underlying and carrying all sacraments and all phenomena and events within the holy, sacramental, and sacred spatial setting of the church is the transformational substantialist procedure in which Christ's humanity from the beginning gets an overlay of divine transformed embodiment. Christ as the divine human being who operates through the office bearers and consecrated icons within the infrastructural spatial setting of the church is day-after-day enacted, employed, applied, and offered by the priesthood to the lay believers within the holy, sacred, and sacramental space of the church.

Outside the holy sacramental and sacred infrastructural setting of the church, many Roman Catholic theologians would speak about Christ as being such an ordinary human that he could catch a cold, get hungry and thirsty, and so on. That many church theologians differ on various points from the everyday "practical theology" of congregational and diocesan experience, usually determined and backed up by the church's central administration and bureaucracy, is not an exclusive Roman Catholic phenomenon. It could be said of nearly all churches, including the Seventh-day Adventist and Reformed churches.

Calvin's and White's intersubstantialist view that God is God and human is human, though very closely connected in one person, Jesus Christ, is miles apart from the transformational substantialist view that something human and something earthly natural could have a transformed divine holy, sacred, and sacramental embodiment. Calvin, for instance, agreed with other Reformers that the Lord's Supper was not meant to be a sacrifice that has to be given to God. He rejected the Mass as a work done by the priests to obtain merits for themselves and others. Calvin described the Mass as a deception of Satan, "a most pestilential error" designed to destroy the Lord's Supper ([1559] 1960d, 18). The Mass is an unbearable blasphemy and dishonor inflicted upon Christ because those who think they have a need to bring daily sacrifices have a need to appoint priests as substitutes for Christ. But they rob Christ of his honor, his eternal priesthood, and his place at the right hand of the Father ([1559] 1960d, 18).

3.10 Consubstantialism

The term, "consubstantiation," emerged around Luther's view of how Christ's body and blood are related to the bread and wine used in the Lord's Supper. The similarity between Luther's view of the humanity of Christ at the cross and his human bodiliness expressed in the bread and wine in the Lord's Supper is remarkable. However, Korff commented one should not overstretch the similarity (1940, 220).

In Luther's view, the human body of Christ is everywhere present, but particularly at the cross and similarly everywhere present, but particularly in the bread and wine of the Holy Communion. In a similar sense, one could add that Christ's human body is everywhere present, but particularly in the human words of the Bible as the Word of God.

In terms of the sweeping sense-making logic that operated among the Protestant Reformers of the sixteenth century, Luther was very original with his view of the human body of Christ as everywhere and overall present, but also present at a specific and particular place, particular spatial sphere at the cross, in the bread and wine, and in the human words of the Bible. In Luther's views, the relationship of Christ's humanity everywhere present and present in a particular way at a particular place is directly related to the relationship of the divinity and the humanity of Christ present in a particular way in a particular spatial entity.

Luther's solution to the problem of Christ being everywhere present, and also in some settings particularly present, is, according to Korff, peculiar. According to Luther, while Christ's body might be everywhere in all creatures, and might be certainly found in stone, fire, water, or a rope, Christ does not want us to grope for him in these things and throw ourselves in the fire and the water or hang ourselves to a rope without the Word. Christ is everywhere present, but he does not want us to grope everywhere for him. Where the Word is, we have to grope for him and understand him correctly (quoted in Korff 1940, 221).

For Luther, it is different whether God is "being there" in the everywhere sense of the word or whether God is "being there for us." Luther appeals to the notion of God determining and ordaining the way by which Christ could be found and encountered at a particular place. The main factor of finding and encountering Christ at a particular place is Luther's use of the working of the Word of God, which permeates the concentrated particular spatial setting and embodiment in which God is present for us in the human body of Christ at the cross, in the bread and wine in the Holy Communion, and in the human words of the Bible. God can only be present in being there for us when the Word permeates the humanity of Christ, the bread and wine, and human words of the Bible. So we do not find Christ in our everyday bread, although he is there, unless he says of particular bread: "This is my body" (Korff 1940, 221).

With regard to his view of the unity of Christ's divine and human nature, Luther has a preference for the formula that "the human being Christ is God." Luther asserts:

> This is the sum total. This is the summary of salvation in which the church triumphs and elates: that a human being is the true God and that only we have in this God and human being eternal life (my translation) (quoted in Korff 1940, 217).

Luther consistently operated with the approach of the two natures of Christ of the church of the past. He linked the divine and human nature of Christ in his writings very closely. Thus, when one says that God is present at this moment for us, one also has to say that Christ the human being is also present (Korff 1940, 216). In the person of Christ, we encounter the true God and the true human being in such a way that in this person, both the divinity and the humanity is one or a thing like a cake, so that one could justifiably say, "This human being is God" (Korff 1940, 217).

According to Luther, Christ is certainly in heaven. However, this should not be thought of as a particular place (*certus locus*), but as an omnipresent heaven (*coelum ubiquitarium*). Christ in his humanity and human body is also omnipresent (Korff 1940, 219). Luther's view of the omnipresence of Christ's humanity and human body elicited heavy reaction from Calvin. Calvin operated with the view that Christ is with his resurrected humanity and body in heaven, where he is engaged as the ongoing mediator, interceding for us. What is of particular importance in this context is that both Calvin and White taught the same doctrine: that Christ is presently in heaven with his resurrected body and mediates as our heavenly Priest before God. However, they do differ in some of the details: The main connecting link between Christ in heaven and us on earth is the Spirit of Christ, the Holy Spirit. Luther has a similar view that the Holy Spirit is Christ present (Nürnberger 2005, 226). The fact that Calvin and the whole reformed tradition did not develop the role of the Spirit into a full-blown emphasis of God's grand act of renewal through Pentecost is only tackled in the twentieth century by reformed theologians, such as Noordmans and Van Ruler becoming aware of the Pentecostal and Charismatic revival in the middle of the century after the turn-of-the-century Azusastreet Pentecostal revival in Los Angeles, California.

Luther wanted believers to accept the words of Jesus when he said, "This is my body," because it is not against Scripture or faith that these words were assigned to Christ's body in the first Lord's Supper by Christ himself. It is also not against Scripture or faith that it should happen in all following the Lord's Supper (Korff 1940, 218). To Luther, the Lord's Supper consisted of a combination of two elements—the divine body and blood permeating the earthly bread and wine. At the cross, in a similar sense, Christ's divinity is permeating Christ's human body.

Calvin negated the notion of the bread becoming in some sense the real body of Christ and the wine being converted into the real blood of the Lord Jesus Christ. While Christ's resurrected body is in heaven, it is Christ's Spirit that feeds the believers with Christ's heavenly body in and through the bread and the wine, which stay just plain bread and wine. As for White, her position is strongly in opposition to that of Luther. White's position also differs from that of Calvin in a sense that she viewed the Lord's Supper mainly as a memorial of Christ's death and resurrection. She saw the purpose of this celebration as a continual reminder to the believer to have complete reliance on the Lord's blood for salvific purposes. To White, the broken bread represented the broken body of the Lord, while the grape juice represented the spilled blood of our Lord. Hence, White is closer to Zwingli in the interpretation above, since she viewed the elements of communion as symbols of the Lord's body and blood (Dederen 2000, 602-606). Another difference is that White believes in using grape juice, as opposed to the aforementioned Reformers, who used real fermented grapes as in alcoholic wine. White describes the Last Supper as follows:

> Christ is still at the table on which the paschal supper has been spread. The unleavened cakes used at the Passover season are before Him. The Passover wine, untouched by fermentation, is on the table. These emblems Christ employs to represent His own unblemished sacrifice. Nothing corrupted by fermentation, the symbol of sin and death, could represent the "Lamb without blemish and without spot" (White [1898] 1948a, 653).

3.11 Epilogue

In Calvin's approach, the duality of the two natures of Christ is set, on one hand, as the combined dual divinely particularized and concentrated divine/human mediating prototype between God and human beings, between heaven and earth, as the mediator that intercedes for us before God. And, on the other, within the biblical historical timeline, Christ is centrally positioned as the divine/human mediating archetype between God's act of creation at the beginning of time and God's act of fulfillment at the end of time, and is therefore simultaneously fully involved in God's acts of creation, reconciliation, renewal, and fulfillment to the end of time.

In Calvin's view, Christ at the right hand of the Father, is the perpetual mediator who continually appears before the Father in his death and resurrection but is simultaneously at the right hand of the Father, the one who obtained dominion over heaven and earth, full of power, and who rules over all things. Christ, in Calvin's view, in his mediatorship is the kingly priest. The prophetship of Christ is de-emphasized in the Calvinian view because its function is assigned to scripture as the inscripturated Christ, whose scriptural bodiliness has to be rightly understood and expounded.

With Calvin, the office of mediation is viewed as transitory. Unlike White, who viewed the limitation that Christ has imposed upon himself by assuming the human nature to be perpetual and thereby rendering himself to be subservient and obsequious to God, Calvin deemed the mediation and submission of Christ to God as transitory:

> Christ, therefore, shall reign until he appears to judge the world, inasmuch as, according to the measure of our feeble capacity, he now connects us with the Father. But when, as partakers of the heavenly glory, we shall see God as he is, then Christ, having accomplished the office of Mediator, shall cease to be the vicegerent of the Father, and will be content with the glory which he possessed before the world was . . . God will then cease to be the head of Christ, and Christ's own Godhead will then shine forth of itself, whereas it is now in a manner veiled (Calvin [1989] 2001b, 418).

In White's approach, *Christ, the family of earth, and the family of heaven are bound together. Christ glorified is our brother. Heaven is enshrined in humanity, and humanity is enfolded in the bosom of infinite love.* Through God's communicative infinite love in Christ, God and human beings are closely connected, concentrated, and contracted, and in Christ emerges the divine/human template of how God is connectively working within his grand acts of creation, reconciliation, renewal, and fulfillment. Christ in and through the divinely set time periods or dispensations from Genesis to Revelation is the central embodiment and manifestation of God's love.

In the ongoing and perpetual sanctuary ministry, the ascension of Christ is that of one who is a divine conqueror. The name "divine conqueror" used for Christ's ascension into heaven is an interesting alternate Christological title that White employed for Christ. Another title expressed by White, in addition to the title of divine conqueror, is that Christ had, by his resurrection, "authenticated Himself as a living Savior." In this self-authentication of Christ, a glorifying majesty and empowering affirmation took place that is ongoing in the processual interceding of the priestly prophet, who, as the resurrected one, can no longer be associated with death, but rather with his glorification within the heavenly cosmos.

With Christ's mediation and priesthood, a different phase of priesthood/mediation continues since there will be no temple or sanctuary, nor will there be any sin that can be deciphered. From White's emphatic suggestion of the retention of Christ's human nature into eternity:

> When God would assure us of His immutable counsel of peace, He gives His only begotten Son to become one of the human family, forever to retain His human nature as a pledge that God will fulfill His word . . . Man's substitute and surety must have man's nature, a connection with the human family whom He was to represent, and, as God's ambassador, He must partake of the divine nature, have a connection with the Infinite, in order to manifest God to the world, and be a mediator between God and man (White [1953] 1985a, 488).

References

Aristotle, 1928. *Topica and De Sophisticis Elenchis*. Oxford: Oxford University Press.

Bainton, R. H. 1992. *Christianity*. New York: American Heritage Inc.

Bakhuizen van den Brink, J. N. 1965. *De Kerk tot Gregorius de Grote*. Vol. 1 of *Handboek der Kerkgeschiedenis*. Den Haag: Bert Bakker / Daamen NV.

Bakhuizen van den Brink, J. N., and W. F. Dankbaar. 1967. *Reformatie en Contra-reformatie*. Vol. 3 of *Handboek der Kerkgeschiedenis*. Den Haag: Bert Bakker / Daamen NV.

Ball, B. W. 1981. *The English Connection: The Puritan Roots of Seventh-day Adventist Belief*. Cambridge: James Clarke.

Barth, K. [1937] 1956. *The Doctrine of the Word of God*, Vol. 1, Part 2. Translated by Thompson, G.T. and Knight, H. *Church Dogmatics*. Edinburgh: T&T Clark.

Barth, K. [1932] 1975. *The Doctrine of the Word of God*, Vol. 1, Part 1. *Church Dogmatics*. Translated by Bromiley, G.W. Edinburgh: T&T Clark.

Bates, J. n.d. *Autobiography*. New Bedford, Connecticut: Press of Benjamin Lindsey.

Battles, F. L., and A. M. Hugo, 1969. *Calvin's Commentary on Seneca's De Clementia*. Leiden: E. J. Brill.

Blazen, I. T. 2000. "Salvation." In *Handbook of Seventh-day Adventist Theology*, 271-313. Hagerstown, Maryland: Review and Herald Publishing Association.

Bouwsma, W. J. 1988. *John Calvin: A Sixteenth-Century Portrait*. New York/Oxford: Oxford University Press.

Brand, L., and L. MachMahon. 2005. *The Prophet and Her Critics*. Nampa: Pacific Press Publishing Association.

Breen, Q. 1968. *John Calvin: A Study in French Humanism*. 2nd ed. Hamden, CT: Archon Books.

Brown, D. 2004. *The Da Vinci Code*. London: Transworld Publishers.

Calvin, J. 1958. *Calvin: Commentaries.* Edited by J. Haroutunian. London: SCM Press.

Calvin, J. [1948] 2001. *Genesis Commentary*. Series editors Alister McGrath and J. I. Packer. USA: Crossway Books. Calvin, J.

Calvin, J. [1559] 1960a. *Institutes of the Christian, Religion. Book I.* Translated by F. L. Battles. Philadelphia: Westminster Press.

———. [1559] 1960b. *Institutes of the Christian Religion. Book II.* Translated by F. L. Battles. Philadelphia: Westminster Press.

———. [1559] 1960c. *Institutes of the Christian Religion. Book III.* Translated by F. L. Battles. Philadelphia: Westminster Press.

———. [1559] 1960d. *Institutes of the Christian Religion. Book IV.* Translated by F. L. Battles. Philadelphia: Westminster Press.

———. 1961. *The Epistles of Paul the Apostle to the Romans and Thessalonians.* Translated by R. Mackenzie, R. Edinburgh: Oliver and Boyd.

———. [1989] 2001a. *Institutes of the Christian Religion. Book I.* Translated by H. Beveridge. Michigan: WM. B. Eerdmans Publishing Company.

———. [1989] 2001b. *Institutes of the Christian Religion. Book II.* Translated by H. Beveridge. Michigan: WM. B. Eerdmans Publishing Company.

Collins, Owen, ed. 1999. *The Classic Bible Commentary.* Wheaton, Illinois: Crossway Books.

Damsteegt, P. G. [1957] 1977. *Foundations of the Seventh-day Adventist Message and Mission.* Grand Rapids, Michigan: Eerdmans Publishing Association.

Dederen, R. 2000. "Christ: His Person and Work." In *Handbook of Seventh-day Adventist* Theology, 160-204. Hagerstown: Review and Herald.

Douglas, J. D. ed. [1962] 1986. *New Bible Dictionary*, Second Edition. Leicester, England: InterVarsity Press.

Edmonson, S. 2004. *Calvin's Christology.* Cambridge: Cambridge University Press.

Ehrman, B. D. 2004. *Truth and Fiction in The Da Vinci Code*. New York: Oxford University Press, Inc.

Encyclopaedia Britannica Volume 8. 15th ed. [1974] 1982c. Chicago: Helen Hemingway Benton.

Flew, A. and Priest, S. eds. 2002. *A Dictionary of Philosophy*. London: Pan Books.

Gamble, R. C. 1992. *An Elaboration of the Theology of CALVIN*. New York: Garland.

Ganoczy, A 1987. *The Young Calvin*. Translated by Foxgrover, D and Provo, W. Philadelphia: Westminster Press.

Ganoczy, A., and S. Scheld, 1982. *Herrschaft—Tugend—Vorsehung, Hermeneutische Deutung und Veröffentlichung handschriftlicher Annotationen Calvins zu sieben Seneca tragödien und den Pharsalia Lucans*. Wiesbaden: Franz Steiner Verlag.

Garlow, J. L. 2006. *The Da Vinci Code Breaker*. Michigan: Baker Publishing Group.

General Conference of Seventh-day Adventists 1988. *Seventh-day Adventists Believe . . .* Washington: All-Africa Publications.

González, J. L. 1984. *The Story of Christianity: Volume 1*. New York: HarperCollins Publishers.

Green, J.P. Sr. 1976. *The Interlinear Bible*. Massachusetts: Hendrickson Publishers

Guthrie, H. H. 1960. *God and History in the Old Testament*. Greenwich, Connecticut: Seabury Press.

Hale, V.A., Saunders, J.P., and Margham, W.G. [1999] (2005). *Collins Dictionary of Biology*. Wrotham, England: HarperCollins Publishers

Harnack, A 1961. *History of Dogma*. Volume IV. Translated by Buchanan, N. New York: Dover Publications.

Haroutunian, J. 1958. *Calvin: Commentaries*. London: S. C. M. Press.

Harris, H. H. 1998. *Fundamentalism and Evangelicals*. Oxford: Clarendon Press.

Hegel [1817] 1959. *Encyclopedia of Philosophy*. Translated by G. E. Meuller. New York: Continuum.

Heussi, K. 1971. *Kompendium der Kirchengeschichte.* Tübingen: J. C. B. Mohr (Paul Siebeck).

Jansen, J. F. 1956. *Calvin's Doctrine of the Work of Christ.* Great Brittan: Camelot.

Kant, I. [1781] 2003. *Critique of Pure Reason.* Translated by John Meikle. New York: Dover Publications.

Kerr, H. T. 1989. *Calvin's Institutes: A New Compend.* Kentucky: John Knox.

Knight, G. R. 2000. *A Search for Identity: The Development of Seventh-day Adventist Beliefs.* Maryland: Review & Herald.

———. 2007. *If I Were the Devil.* Hagerstown, MD: Review and Herald.

Korff, F.W.A 1940. *Christologie. De Leer van het Komen Gods. Volume 1.* Nijkerk: GF Callenbach.

Loughborough, J. N. [1905] 1972. *The Great Second Advent Movement: Its Rise and Progress.* Washington, DC: Review and Herald Publishing Assn/New York: Arno Press.

Lutzer, E. W. 2005. *The Da Vinci Deception.* S1: Tyndale House Publishers, Inc.

MacCulloch, D. 2009. *A History of Christianity.* England: Penguin Books Ltd.

Moon, J 2003a. The Adventist Trinity Debate, Part 1: Historical Overview. *Andrews University Seminary Studies,* Vol. 41, No. 1, 113-129. Berrien Springs, MI: Andrews University Press.

Moon, J. 2003b. The Adventist Trinity Debate, Part 2: The Role of Ellen G. White. *Andrews University Seminary Studies,* 41 No. 2, 275-292. Berrien Springs, MI: Andrews University Press.

Nürnberger, K 2005. *Martin Luther's message for us today. A perspective from the South.* Pietermaritzburg: Cluster Publications.

Oberman, H. A. 1986. *The Dawn of the Reformation.* Edinburgh: T&T Clark.

Oberman, H. A. 1991. *Initia Calvini: The Matrix of Calvin's Reformation.* Amsterdam: Noord-Hollancsche.

Ostow, M 1990. *The Fundamentalist Phenomenon*. Michigan: Eerdmans Publishing Co.

Pagels, E. 1989. *The Gnostic Gospels*. New York: Vintage Book.

Pagels, E 1994. Interview transcript with Michael Philips. http://media.barnesandnoble.com/?fr_chl

Palmer, E. H. 1980. *The Five Points of Calvinism*. USA: Baker Book House.

Partee, C. 2008. *The Theology of John Calvin*. Louisville, Kentucky: Westminster John Knox Press.

Plantak, Z. 1998. *The Silent Church. Human rights and Adventist Social Ethics*. London: Macmillan.

Porter, G. R., and M. Greengrass, 1983. *Documents of Modern History*. London: Edward Arnold.

Riley, G.J. 1997. *One Jesus Many Christs*. San Francisco: Harper Collins.

Scofield, C. I. [1967] 2005. *The Scofield Study Bible, New King James Version*. UK: Oxford University Press.

The Amplified Bible 1987. Michigan: Zondervan Corporation.

The Holy Bible: King James Version 1976. North Carolina: Bible House.

The Holy Bible: New International Version [1978] 2001. South Africa: Bible Society of South Africa.

Torrance, T. F. 1988. *The Hermeneutics of John Calvin*. Edinburgh: Scottish Academic Press.

Van Niekerk, E. 1984. *Methodological Aspects in Karl Barth's Church Dogmatic's*. DTh Thesis. UNISA: Pretoria.

———. 2005. "Wholesome and Dynamic Sense Making Approaches in the Transfer of Doctrines and Theories of Faith." In *Studia Historiae Ecclesiasticae*, Vol. 31, Nr 2, 401-425.

———. 2009b. The Dual Story Line of Calvin's Sense-Making Approach. In *Studia Historiae Ecclesiasticae*, Vol 35, Nr 2, 33-55.

Venden, M. 1996. *Never without an Intercessor. The Good News about the Judgment*. Ontario: Pacific Press Publishing Association.

Vernon 2008. *Humanism*. USA: McGraw-Hill Companies, Inc.

Vives, J. L. 1979. *Against the Pseudodialecticians (Contra Pseudodialecticos)*. Translated by Guerlac, R. Boston: Reidel.

Vos, G. 1906. "Christian Faith and the Truthfulness of Bible History." *The Princeton Theological Review* 4: 289-302

Waggoner, E. J. 1890. *Christ and His Righteousness*. Clarksville, AR: Pathway Publishers.

Walker, W. 1985. *A History of the Christian Church*. 4th ed. New York: Charles Scribner & Sons.

Waterworth, J 1848. *The canons and decrees of the sacred and oecumenical Council of Trent 1545-1564*. Edited and translated by Waterworth, J. London: Dolman.

Weber, O. [1962] 1981-1983. *Foundations of Dogmatics*. Grand Rapids, Michigan: Eerdmans.

Whidden, W. 1997. "Arianism, Adventism and Methodism: The Healing of Trinitarian Teaching and Soteriology." A Paper Presented to The Tenth Oxford, MI (USA) Institute of Methodist Theol. Studies Working Group: History of Wesleyan Traditions.

White, A. L. 1985. *Ellen G White. The Early Years, Volume 1, 1827–1862*. Washington, DC: Review and Herald Publishing Association.

White, E. G [1882] 1945a. *Early Writings*. Washington, DC: Review and Herald Publishing Association.

———. 1884. *The Spirit of Prophecy, Volume Four. The Sanctuary*. Oakland, California: Pacific Press; Battle Creek, Michigan: Review and Herald.

———. [1888] 1987. *Miscellaneous Collections. The Ellen G. White 1888 Materials. Letter 81, to A. O. Olsen, 1896.*

———. [1888] 1990a. *The Great Controversy*. Florida: Laymen for Religious Liberty.

———. [1890] 1958a. *Patriarchs and Prophets*. California: Pacific Press Publishing Association.

———. [1893] 1982. *Steps to Christ*. England: The Stanborough Press.

———. [1898] 1948a. *Desire of Ages*. 12th ed. California: Pacific Press Publishing Association.

———. [1900] 1941. *Christ's Object Lessons*. California: Pacific Press Publishing Association
———. 1906. "Come Out and Be Separate." In *Testimonies for the Church Containing Messages of Warning and Instruction to Seventh-day Adventists*. S1: White Estates.
———. 1911. *Acts of the Apostles*. Washington, DC: Review and Herald Publishing Association.
———. 1913. *Counsels to Parents, Teachers, and Students*. Washington, DC: Review and Herald Publishing Association.
———. [1917] 1943. *Prophets and Kings*. Mountain View, California: Pacific Press Publishing Association.
———. [1923] 1962. *Testimonies To Ministers and Gospel Workers*. California: Pacific Press Publishing Association.
———. 1940. *Counsels on Stewardship*. California: Pacific Press Publishing Association.
———. [1946] 1970. *Evangelism*. Washington, DC: Review and Herald Publishing Association
———. [1953] 1985. *Christian Leadership*. California: Pacific Press Publishing Association.
———. [1953] 1985a. *S.D.A. Bible Commentary, Volume 7A*. Washington, DC: Review and Herald Publishing Association.
———. 1955. *Sons and Daughters of God*. Washington, DC: Review and Herald Publishing Association
———.1956b. *S.D.A. Bible Commentary, Volume 6*. Washington, DC: Review and Herald Publishing Association.
———.1957.*S.D.A. Bible Commentary, Volume 7*.Washington, DC: Review and Herald Publishing Association.
———. 1958b. *Selected Messages: Book 1*. Washington, DC: Review and Herald Publishing Association.
———. [1961]1989. *Our High Calling. An Advocate with the Father*. Hagerstown, Maryland: Review and Herald Publishing Association.
———. 1964. *That I May Know Him. Power of Obedience*. Washington, DC: Review and Herald Publishing Association.

———. 1979. *Faith and Works*. Washington, DC: Review and Herald Publishing Association.
———. 1982b. *The Upward Look*. California: Pacific Press Publishing Association.
———. 1988. *Lift Him Up*. Washington, DC: Review and Herald.
———. 1992. *Last Day Events*. Boise, Idaho: Pacific Press Publishing Association.
———. 1995. *Ye Shall Receive Power*. Washington, D. C: Review and Herald Publishing Association.
White, E. G.: Periodicals
———. "The Word Made Flesh." *Review and Herald,* April, 5 1906.
———. "Watchfulness and Prayer." *Review and Herald,* October 11, 1881.
———. "Experience and Views." *Review and Herald,* July 21, 1851.
———. "God's Purpose for Us." *Signs of the Times,* May 29, 1901.
———. "Obedience Better Than Sacrifice." *Signs of the Times,* September 14, 1882.
White, J. 1852. *Review and Herald, August, 5 1852*. Washington, DC: Review and Herald Publishing Association.

ELECTRONIC REFERENCES:

http://atsjats.org/site/1/podcast/06_Trinity_Moon_Quest_Biblical_Trinity.mp3 (20/01/2014)
http://de.wikipedia.org/wiki/Ernst_Bloch (20/01/2014)
http://ecumenicity.blogspot.com/2007/09/gnostic-roots-of-heresy.html (20/04/2010)
http://en.wikipedia.org/wiki/Institutes_of_the_Christian_Religion (20/01/2014)
http://en.wikipedia.org/wiki/John_Calvin (20/01/2014)
http://members.home.nl/cgf.de.jong/index.html (20/01/2014)
http://www.adherents.com/people/ pm/William_McKinley (20/04/2010)
http://www.archive.org/details/lecturesonscien00grahgoog (20/01/2014)

http://www.cresourcei.org/creeddordt (20/04/2010)
http:// www.earlychristianwritings.com/text/Ignatius =smyrnaeans=longer.html (20/04/2010)
http://www.god-head.com/index.php?option=com (20/04/2010)
http://www.pacificpress.com/index.php?pgName =splSearch&sku=0816323402 (20/04/2010)
http://uir.unisa.ac.za/bitstream/handle/10500/4210/thesis_jones_p.pdf.txt?sequence=3
http://www.presenttruthmag.com/7dayadventist/Waggoner/1.html (20/01/2014)
http://www.sdanet.org/atissue/books/webster/ccac03-1.htm (20/01/2014)
http://www.statemaster.com/encyclopedia/E.-J.-Waggoner (20/01/2014)
http://www.trend.infopartisan.net/trd0407/t020407.html (20/01/2014)

ADDITIONAL SOURCES:

Alighieri, D. [2002] 2005. *Inferno*. New York: The Modern Library.
Andreasen, M. L. 1942. *The Sabbath, Which Day and Why?* Washington D.C: Review and Herald Publishing Association.
Andreasen, M. L. 1949. *God's Holy Day*. Washington D.C: Review and Herald Publishing Association.
Baigent, M., R. Leigh, and H. Lincon, 1996. *The Holy Blood and the Holy Grail*. Great Britain: Cox & Wyman Ltd.
Bakhuizen van den Brink, J. N., and W. F. Dankbaar. 1968. *De Kerk sedert de zeventiende eeuw*. Vol. 4 of *Handboek der Kerkgeschiedenis*..Den Haag: Bert Bakker / Daamen NV.
Barr, J. 1977. *Fundamentalism*. London: SCM.
Beardsley, F. G. 1943. *Religious Progress through Religious Revivals*. New York: American Tract Society.
Biéler, A. 2005. *Calvin's Economic and Social Thought*. Translated J. Greig. Geneva: WCC Publications.
Bird, H. S. 1961. *Theology of Seventh-day Adventism*. Grand Rapids: Eerdman.

Bloch, E. 1959. *Das Prinzip Hoffnung*. Frankfurt: Suhrkamp Verlag.

Bodanis, D. [2000] 2001. *E=mc^2: A Biography of the World's Most Famous Equation*. Great Britain: Macmillan. *Canons of Dort, First Point of Doctrine, Article 7.*

Brunner, E. 1939. *Man in Revolt. A Christian Anthropology.* Translated by O.Wyon. London: Lutterworth Press.

Calvin, J. (1536) 1975. *Institution of the Christian Religion. Embracing Almost the Whole Sum of Piety and Whatever Is Necessary To Know the Doctrine of salvation: A Work Most Worthy to be Read by All Persons Zealous for Piety.* Translated by F. L. Battles. Atlanta: John Knox Press.

———. [1989] 2001c. *Institutes of the Christian Religion. Book III*. Translated by H. Beveridge. Michigan: WM. B. Eerdmans Publishing Company.

———. [1989] 2001d. *Institutes of the Christian Religion Book IV*. Translated by H. Beveridge. Michigan: WM. B. Eerdmans Publishing Company.

———. 1963. *Calvin's Commentaries. The Epistle of Paul the Apostle to the Hebrews and The First and Second Epistles of St Peter.* Translated by W. B. Johnston. Edinburgh: Oliver and Boyd.

———. 2005. *John Calvin: God the Creator, God the Redeemer. Institutes of the Christian Religion*. Translated by Henry Beveridge. Gainesville, Florida: Bridge-Logos Publishers.

———. 2000. *Jeremiah Commentary*. Series editors Alister McGrath and J. I. Packer. USA: Crossway Books.

———. 1980. *John Calvin's Sermons on the Ten Commandments.* Edited and Translated by B. W. Farley. Grand Rapids, Michigan: Baker Book House.

Canale, F. L. 2000. "Doctrine of God." In *Handbook of Seventh-day Adventist* Theology, 105-159. Hagerstown, Maryland: Review and Herald Publishing Association.

Carson, D. A. 1996. *The Gagging of God: Christianity Confronts Pluralism*. Grand Rapids, Michigan: Zondervan Publishing House.

Coombs, N. 1972. *The Immigrant Heritage of America.* [S l]: Twayne Press.

Cottret, B. 2000. *CALVIN: A Biography*. Grand Rapids, Michigan: WB Eerdmans Publishing Company: Edinburgh: T&T Clark.

Dederen, R. 1992. "On Inspiration and Biblical Authority." In *Adventist Theological Society Occasional Papers. Volume 1*, edited by F. Holbrook and L.Van Dolson, 91-104. Adventist Theological Society Publications: Berrien Springs, Michigan.

De Jong, C. G. F. 1987. "John Forbes (ca. 1568–1634)." PhD diss. RU: Groningen.

Delafiel, D. A. to P. C. Drewer on June 24, 1981. E. G. White Estates.

Douglas, J. D., ed. 1990. *The New Greek English Interlinear New Testament*. Illinois: Tyndale House Publishing.

Douglass, H. E. 1998. *Messenger of the Lord: The Prophetic Ministry of Ellen G. White*. Nampa, ID: Pacific Press.

Encyclopaedia Britannica Volume 1. 15th ed. [1768] 1982a. Chicago: Helen Hemingway Benton.

Encyclopaedia Britannica Volume 16. 15th ed. [1768] 1982b. Chicago: Helen Hemingway Benton.

Froom, L. R. 1946-1954a. *Prophetic Faith of Our Fathers*. Vol. 3. Washington, DC: Review and Herald.

———. 1946-1954b. *Prophetic Faith of Our Fathers*. Vol. 4. Washington, DC: Review and Herald.

———. 1948. *Historical Development of Prophetic Interpretation*. Washington, DC: Review and Herald.

Gane, L. and Piero, eds. 2008. *Introducing Nietzsche: A Graphic Guide*. Thriplow, Cambridge: Icon Books Ltd. In *The Seventh Day*, edited by B. Herndon. 1960. New York: McGraw-Hill.

Gaustad, E. S., ed. 1974. *The Rise of Adventism: Religion and Society in Mid-Nineteenth-Century America*. New York: Harper & Row.

General Conference Bulletin. 1897. Seventh-day Adventist Church.

General Conference Bulletin. 1899. Seventh-day Adventist Church.

Gould, S. J. 1999. *Rock of Ages: Science and Religion in the Fullness of Life*. New York: Ballantine Publishing Group

Gould, P. M. 2007. *The Two Tasks of the Christian Scholar: Redeeming the Soul, Redeeming the Mind.* USA: Good News & Crossway.

Graham, S. [1839] 1849. *Lectures on the Science of Human Life.* Oxford: Boston, Marsh, Capen, Lyon & Webb.

Griffin, E., ed. 2006. *John Calvin: Selections from His Writings.* USA: HarperCollins Publishers.

Gulley, N. R. 2003. *Systematic Theology: Prolegomena.* Berrien Springs, Michigan: Andrews University Press.

Hesselink, I. J. 1997. *Calvin's First Catechism. A Commentary. Columbia Series in Reformed Theology.* Kentucky: Westminister John Knox Press.

Himes, J. V. 1842. *Views of the Prophecies and Prophetic Chronology Selected from Manuscripts of William Miller.* Boston: J. V. Himes.

Holder, R.W. 2006. *John Calvin and the Grounding of Interpretation: Calvin's First Commentaries.* London: T&T Clark.

Hollingworth, R. 1656. *The Holy Ghost on the Bench.* London: Luke Fawn.

Irwin, C. H. 1909. *John Calvin: The Man and his Work.* London: The Religious Tract Society.

Jamison, T. H. 1955. *A Prophet among You.* Mountain View, California: Pacific Press.

Johnsson, W.G. 2000. Biblical Apocalyptic, 784-814, in *The Handbook of Seventh-day Adventist Theology.* Hagerstown: Review & Herald.

Knight, G. R. 1993. *Millennial Fever and the End of the World.* Boise, Idaho: Pacific Press.

———. 1998. *Ellen White's World.* Hagerstown, MD: Review and Herald.

Land, G., ed. 1987. *The World of Ellen G. White.* Hagerstown, MD: Review and Herald.

Loughborough, J. N. [1905] 1972. *The Great Second Advent Movement: Its Rise and Progress.* Washington, DC: Review and Herald Publishing Assn/New York: Arno Press.

McGrath, A. E. 1987. *The Intellectual Origins of the European Reformation.* Oxford: Blackwell.

McGrath, A. [1990] 2000. *A Life of John Calvin*. Massachusetts: Blackwell Publishers.

Macinnis, P. 2008. *Mr Darwin's Incredible Shrinking World*. Millers Point, Australia: Pier 9.

Mckim, D. K. 2004. *The Cambridge Companion to John Calvin*. Cambridge: Cambridge University Press.

McLoughlin, W. G. 1974. *Revivalism*. In *The Rise of Adventism: Religion and Society in Mid-Nineteenth-Century America*, edited by E. S. Gaustad. New York: Harper & Row.

Miller, W. 1845. *Apology and Defence*. Corvallis, Oregon: Seventh-day Adventist.

Montefiore, S. S. 2005. *Speeches That Changed the World*. London: Quercus Publishing Ltd.

Muller, R. A. 1986. *Christ and the Decree. Christology and Predestination in Reformed Theology from Calvin to Perkins*. Durham, North Carolina: Labyrinth Press.

Muller, R. A. 2003. *After Calvin. Studies in the Development of a Theological Tradition*. Oxford: Oxford University Press.

Neufeld, D. F., ed. 1960. *Seventh-day Adventist Bible Dictionary*. Washington D.C: Review and Herald Publishing Association.

Nigrini, J. 2007. *Kenosis and Identities: Pneumatological Pointers*. PhD Diss. Pretoria: Unisa.

Noordmans, O. [1934] 1956. *Herschepping. Beknopte dogmatische handleiding voor godsdienstige toespraken en besprekingen*. Zeist. 2nd impression Amsterdam.

Nutall, G. H. 1947. *The Holy Spirit in Puritan Faith and Experience*. Chicago: University of Chicago Press.

Olson, R. E. 1999. *The Story of Christian Theology: Twenty Centuries of Tradition and Reform*. Downers Grove, Illinois: InterVarsity Press.

Pannenberg, W. 1988. *The Apostle's Creed*. SCM: London.

Paulien, J. K. 2005. *Understanding Scripture: An Adventist Approach. The Hermeneutics of Biblical Apocalyptic*. George W. Reid, ed. Silver Springs, Maryland: Biblical Research Institute.

Pfandl, G. 1992. *The Time of the End in the Book of Daniel*. Berrien Springs, Michigan: Adventist Theological Society.

Plato. 2005. *The Laws.* Translated by Hale, Saunders, and Margham. USA: Penguin Classics.

Rebok, D. E. 1956. *Believe His Prophets.* Washington, DC: Review and Herald.

Reid, G. W., et al. 2000. *Handbook of Seventh-day Adventist Theology.* Hangerstown, Maryland: Review and Herald Publishing Association.

Roberts, M. D. 2007. *Can We Trust the Gospels?* Illinois: Crossway Books.

Russell, H. 2009. *The Politics of Hope: The Words of Barack Obama.* Cape Town, South Africa: Zebra Press.

Sawyer, M. J. 2006. *The Survivor's Guide to Theology.* Grand Rapids, Michigan: Zondervan.

Scofield, C. I. [1967] 2005. *The Scofield Study Bible, New King James Version.* UK: Oxford University Press.

Selderhuis H. J. 2009. *John Calvin: A Pilgrim's Life.* Illinois: InterVarsity Press.

Seventh-day Adventists Answers to Questions on Doctrine. 1957. Washington, D.C: Review and Herald Publishing Association.

Seventh-day Adventists Believe. 2005. Silver Spring, Maryland: The Stanborough Press Ltd.

Seventh-day Adventist Church Yearbook, Volume 7. Battle Creek, Michigan: Review and Herald Publishing Association.

Shea, W. H. 1992. *Selected Studies on Prophetic Interpretation.* Rev. ed. Silver Spring, Maryland: Biblical Research Institute.

Smalley, B. 1983. *The Study of the Bible in the Middle Ages.* Oxford: Basil Blackwell.

Smay, L. J. U. 1915. *The Sanctuary and the Sabbath.* Cleveland: Evangelical Association.

Soanes, C., ed. 2002. *Oxford English Dictionary.* New York: Oxford University Press.

Standish, C. D., and R. R. Standish. 1998. *Adventism Vindicated.* Rapidan, VA: Hartland Publications.

Sthrehle, S. 1995. *The Catholic Roots of the Protestant Gospel. Encounter between the Middle Ages and the Reformation.* Leiden: E. J. Brill.

Stump, E., and N. Kretzmann, eds. 2002. *The Cambridge Companion to Augustine.* New
York: Cambridge University Press.

Thompson, A. 2005 *Escape from the Flames: How Ellen White Grew from Fear to Joy—and Helped Me Do It Too.* Nampa, ID: Pacific Press.

Thompson, A. 2009. *Beyond Common Ground: Why Liberals and Conservatives Need Each Other.* California: Pacific Press Publishing Association.

Thornton J. F. and S. B. Varenne. 2006. *John Calvin. Steward of God's Covenant, Selected Writings.* USA: Vintage Spiritual Classics.

Ussher, J. 2006. The Annals of the World. Green Forest, Arizona: Master Books.

Van Buren, P. 1957. *Christ in Our Place: The Substitutionary Character of Calvin's Doctrine of Reconciliation.* Edinburgh: Oliver & Boyd.

Van Niekerk, E. 2006. "The Church as Golden Calf in History and the Meandering Processes of the Commonwealth of God." In *Studia Historiae Ecclesiasticae*, Vol. 32. Nr 3, 315-405.

———. 2009. *Faith, Philosophy and Science.* TL 501/2009. Unisa: Pretoria.

Van Peursen, C. A. 1966. *LICHAAM—ZIEL—GEEST. Inleiding tot een fenomenologische antropologie.* Utrecht: Erven J Bijleveld.

Walker, A. 1953. *The Law and the Sabbath.* Nashville: Southern Publishers Association.

Water, M., ed. 2004. Parallel Classic Commentary on the New Testament. Chattanooga, Tennessee: AMG Publishers.

Webster, E. C. [1927] 1984. *Crosscurrents in Adventist Christology.* New York: Peter Lang Publishing, Inc.

Woolf, H. B., ed. 1979. *Webster's New Collegiate Dictionary.* Springfield, Massachusetts, USA: G. & C. Merriam Company.

Wendel, F. [1963] 1968. *Calvin: Origins and Development of His Religious Thought.* Translated by P. Mairet. New York: Harper & Row.

Whale, J. S. 1960. *Victor and Victim*. Cambridge: Cambridge University Press.

White, A. L.[1984] 1885-1886. *Ellen G White. The Lonely Years, Volume 3, 1876–1891*. Washington, DC: Review and Herald Publishing Association.

White, E. G. [1827-1915] 1996. *The Truth About Angels. Angels at Christ's Baptism and in the Wilderness*. Boice, Idaho: Pacific Press Publishing Association.

———. [1855-1868] 1948a. *Testimonies for the Church Volume 1*. California: Pacific Press Publishing Association.

———. [1858-1871] 1948b. *Testimonies for the Church Volume 2*. California: Pacific Press Publishing Association.

———. [1858] 1945b. *Spiritual Gifts Vol. I-II. The Trial of Christ*. Battle Creek, Michigan: James White.

———. 1870. *The Spirit of Prophecy, Volume One. The Creation*. Oakland, California: Pacific Press; Battle Creek, Michigan: Review and Herald.

———. [1876-1881] 1948d. *Testimonies for the Church, Volume 4*. California: Pacific Press Publishing Association.

———. 1877a. *The Spirit of Prophecy, Volume Two*. Oakland, California: Pacific Press; Battle Creek, Michigan: Review and Herald.

———. [1882-1889] 1948e. *Testimonies for the Church, Volume 5*. California: Pacific Press Publishing Association.

———. [1892] 1915. *Gospel Workers*. California: Pacific Press Publishing Association.

———. [1893] 1923. *Christian Education*. Nashville, Tennessee: Southern Publishing Association.

———. [1901] 1985. *Reflecting Christ*. Washington, DC: Review and Herald Publishing Association.

———. 1903. *Education*. Washington, DC: Review and Herald Publishing Association.

———. [1905] 1990. *Ministry of Healing*. Silversprings, Maryland: Better Living Publishers, a trademark of ASI Missions Inc.

———. 1910-1915. *Present Truth and Review and Herald. Articles, Volume 6*. Washington, D.C: Review and Herald Publishing association.

———. [1915] 1943. *Life Sketches of Ellen G. White*. California: Pacific Press Publishing Association.

———. 1923a. *Counsels on Health*. Washington, DC: Review and Herald Publishing Association.

———. 1923b. *Fundamentals of Christian Education*. California: Pacific Press Publishing Association.

———. [1940] 1922. *Christian Experience and Teachings of Ellen G. White*. Mountain view, California: Pacific Press Publishing Association.

———. 1945c. *Spiritual Gifts Vol. III-IV*. Michigan: Edwards Brothers.

———. 1946. *Counsels to Writers and Editors*. Nashville: Southern Publishing Association.

———. 1952. *Welfare Ministry*. Washington, D.C: Review and Herald Publishing Association.

———. 1953. *Colporteur Ministry*. Mountain View, California: Pacific Press Publishing Association.

———. 1956a. *S.D.A. Bible Commentary, Volume 5*. Washington, DC: Review and Herald Publishing Association.

———. [1958] 1973. *The Faith I Live By*. Washington, DC: Review and Herald Publishing Association.

———. 1958c. "The 'Holy Flesh' Doctrine." In *Selected Messages: Book 2*. Washington, DC. Review and Herald Publishing Association.

———. 1967. *In Heavenly Places. Glory Indescribable*. Washington, DC: Review and Herald Publishing Association.

———. 1973. *God's Amazing Grace. Christ is Priest upon the Throne*. Washington, DC: Review and Herald Publishing Association.

———. 1976. *Maranatha: The Lord is Coming. Your case Coming Up!*. Washington, DC: Review and Herald Publishing Association.

———. 1977a. *Mind, Character, and Personality, Volume 1*. California: Pacific Press Publishing Association.

———. 1977b. *Mind, Character, and Personality, Volume 2.* California: Pacific Press Publishing Association.
———. 1980. *Selected Messages: Book 3.* Washington, DC: Review and Herald Publishing Association.
———. 1981. *Manuscript Releases, Volume One, Nos. 19-96, MR No. 24, E. G. White Comments on Daniel 2.* Washington, DC: Review and Herald Publishing Association.
———. 1987a. *Manuscript Releases, Volume Two, Nos. 97-161, MR No. 108, How to Study the Bible.* Washington, DC: Review and Herald Publishing Association.
———. 1990b. *Manuscript Releases, Volume Five, Nos. 260-346, MR No. 320, Typical E.G. White Materials.* Washington, DC: Review and Herald Publishing Association.

WHITE, E. G.: PERIODICALS

———. "Tempted in All Points." *The Bible Echo,* July 23, 1900.
———. "Need of Caution." *The Gospel Herald,* August 1, 1899.
———. "Union with Christ." *Review and Herald,* December 13, 1887.
———. "Christ Prayed for Unity Among His Disciples." *Review and Herald,* March 11, 1890.
———. "The Science of Salvation the First of Sciences." *Review and Herald,* December 1, 1891.
———. "The Remnant Church Not Babylon." *Review and Herald,* September 12, 1893.
———. "Resistance to Light. *No. 3.*" *Signs of the Times,* August 29, 1900.
White, W. C. [1911] 1959. Statement to the General Conference Council, October 31, 1911. In *Note and Papers Concerning Ellen G. White Publications.*
Wilcox, M. F. 1944. *The Testimony of Jesus.* Washington D.C: Review & Herald Publishing Association.

Lightning Source UK Ltd.
Milton Keynes UK
UKOW03f1946120417
298994UK00001B/117/P

9 781628 577426